Everyday Life:
ANCIENT TIMES

WITH CROSS-CURRICULAR ACTIVITIES IN EACH CHAPTER

WALTER A. HAZEN

A GOOD YEAR BOOK™

GOOD YEAR BOOKS

Tucson, Arizona

Photo Credits

Front & back cover: All images owned by Good Year Books. 2: Greek bride, Bridgeman Art Library. 4: Etruscan sculpture, Bridgeman Art Library. 5: Tutankhamen's throne, Bridgeman Art Library. 10: Model hut, Bridgeman Art Library. 12: Roman house, Bridgeman Art Library. 18: Egyptian cosmetic spoon, Bridgeman Art Library. 20: Greek statue, Bridgeman Art Library. 26: Stone relief, Bridgeman Art Library. 28: Corinthian vase, Bridgeman Art Library. 29: Chinese market, Bridgeman Art Library. 34: Egyptian hunting scene, Good Year Books. 36: Stadium at Olympia, Bridgeman Art Library. 42: Burial mask of Tutankhamen, Good Year Books. 44: Bronze figurine, Bridgeman Art Library. 45: Fresco, Bridgeman Art Library. 50: Tablet of trireme, Bridgeman Art Library. 52: Appian Way, Bridgeman Art Library. 58: Cuneiform writing, Bridgeman Art Library. 59: Tomb painting, Good Year Books. 61: Statue of Athena, Bridgeman Art Library. 66: Hammurabi, Bridgeman Art Library. 68: Ruins of Athenian Assembly, Bridgeman Art Library. 69: Mosaic of Emperor Justinian, Bridgeman Art Library. 74: Egyptian relief, Bridgeman Art Library. 76: Bust of Hippocrates, Bridgeman Art Library. 77: Chinese acupuncture, Bridgeman Art Library. 82: Pyramids at Gizeh, Good Year Books. 84: Parthenon, Bridgeman Art Library. 85: Colosseum in Rome, Bridgeman Art Library.

Dedication

To Martha, Jordan, and Allison.

Acknowledgments

Grateful acknowledgment is extended to Roberta Dempsey, Editorial Director at Good Year Books, who patiently guided me through this addition to the "Everyday Life" series. Without her advice and support, this book would not have been possible.

I would also like to thank Helen Fisher, Publisher at Good Year Books, for giving me the opportunity to continue the "Everyday Life" series. Her support and confidence in me is likewise appreciated.

Good Year Books

are available for most basic curriculum subjects plus many enrichment areas. For more Good Year Books, contact your local bookseller or educational dealer. For a complete catalog with information about other Good Year Books, please contact:

Good Year Books
P. O. Box 91858
Tucson, Arizona 85752-1858
1-800-511-1530
www.goodyearbooks.com

Editor: Roberta Dempsey
Cover Design: Ronan Design
Interior Design: Dan Miedaner

Printed in the United States of America.

ISBN-10: 1-59647-058-5
ISBN-13: 978-1-59647-058-3

1 2 3 4 5 6 7 8 9 - BN - 07 06 05

Table of Contents

Introduction   1

Chapter 1—**Marriage and Family Life**   **2**
    Research the Ancient World   6
    Recall Information You Have Read   7
    Fill in a Venn Diagram   8
    Use Your Critical Thinking Skills   9

Chapter 2—**Housing**   **10**
    Make a Shoe Box Diorama   14
    Use Context Clues to Complete Sentences   15
    Distinguish between Sentences and Fragments   16
    Solve Some Ancient Housing Word Problems   17

Chapter 3—**Clothing and Appearance**   **18**
    Solve a Clothing Puzzle   22
    Draw a Picture   23
    Name Those Synonyms   24
    Write a Time Travel Dialogue   25

Chapter 4—**Food and Drink**   **26**
    Make False Statements True   30
    Write a Letter to the Editor   31
    Make a Food Mobile   32
    Search Out Some Food Facts   33

Chapter 5—**Fun and Amusements**   **34**
    Write a Lead Paragraph for *The Roman Times*   38
    Evaluate Leisure Activities   39
    Fill in a Venn Diagram   40
    Correct Erroneous Petronius's Math   41

Chapter 6—**Classes and Occupations**   **42**
    Name Those Ancient Persons   46
    Distinguish between Fact and Opinion   47
    Make an Outline   48
    Play the Devil's Advocate   49

Table of Contents *continued*

Chapter 7— **Transportation and Communication**   **50**

Create a Bar Graph of Your Own   54

Solve a Transportation Puzzle   55

Keep a Traveler's Diary   56

Compare and Contrast Two Eras   57

Chapter 8— **Education and Religion**   **58**

Use Your Critical Thinking Skills   62

Compare Ancient and Modern Schools   63

Participate in a Skit   64

Unscramble and Identify Nouns   65

Chapter 9— **Law and Justice**   **66**

Write Your Opinions   70

Write a Letter to the Editor   71

Make False Statements True   72

Complete a Before and After Page   73

Chapter 10— **Health and Medicine**   **74**

Write Meanings of Vocabulary Words   78

Interpret a Bar Graph   79

Create a Dialogue   80

Write an Essay   81

Chapter 11— **Art and Architecture**   **82**

Research One of the Seven Wonders   86

Create a Bulletin Board Display   87

Write a Letter   88

Recall Information You Have Read   89

Answers to Activities   **90**

Additional Resources   **92**

From *Everyday Life: Ancient Times* © 2006 Good Year Books.

Introduction

Strange as it may seem, most of human history has taken place in ancient times. Some 6,000 years have passed since early cities appeared in Egypt, Mesopotamia, India, and China. All but about 1,500 of those years are included in what is termed "ancient history."

It therefore seems appropriate that we know something about the lives and achievements of the many ancient peoples on whose thoughts and accomplishments our own civilization is based. I speak primarily of the Egyptians, the Mesopotamians, the Greeks, and the Romans, and it is on these groups that *Everyday Life: Ancient Times* focuses. Although each chapter mentions life in ancient India and China, the emphasis is always on the former civilizations.

Because of space limitations, the many peoples whose civilizations rose and fell in the area between the Tigris and Euphrates rivers of the Middle East are, for the most part, referred to collectively as "Mesopotamians" and are generally treated as one group. For the same reason, the highly developed civilizations of the various Indian tribes in what later became Central and South America, as well as a number of advanced African civilizations south of Egypt, are not covered in this book. Another book would be required to address these deserving ancient peoples.

As with previous Everyday Life books, *Everyday Life: Ancient Times* does not dwell on governments and leaders. Nor does it discuss wars, battles, natural resources, and other topics covered in general history texts. Instead, it centers on everyday life: how ancient peoples thought, what they ate, what they wore, what their houses were like, and how they looked at marriage and family life. It is a book you should enjoy.

Walter A. Hazen

CHAPTER I

Marriage and Family Life

If you could be whisked back to ancient times by way of a time machine, you would naturally find life very different from your life today. Houses would be different, clothing would be different, and what people did for fun and amusement would be different. So would their views on marriage and the home. Because marriage and family life form the cornerstone of any society, it is here that we begin our study of ancient times. As you read the following pages, you will be introduced to some unusual customs and beliefs. Some will shock you; others will probably make you laugh. But every one should hold your attention and interest to the end.

A young Greek bride readies herself for her wedding; from a fifth-century BC vase painting.

Marriage in ancient societies was, for the most part, a prearranged affair. The father of the bride-to-be struck a deal with either a professional matchmaker or with the prospective groom's family, a suitable dowry was agreed upon, and the young lady in question was officially betrothed. There was no dating involved and often no courtship. In most cases, the girl never saw her future husband until the day of the wedding. She could only hope that he turned out to be kind and not abusive.

Nowhere were ancient views concerning marriage and the home more firmly established than in Greece. In the various Greek city-states, women had different rights. In Athens, the husband ruled supreme and the wife's place was in the home. The typical wife had no rights and did not participate in public affairs, except for a few religious festivals or funerals. She could not own a business or inherit property. She was not even allowed to join her husband in entertaining guests. When her husband had male friends over, the Athenian wife was expected to retire to the back of the house and stay out of sight. In Sparta, women fared much better. For example, they could read and write, unlike other Greek women, and could own property.

But this is only the beginning! In ancient Greece, romantic love was looked upon as a form of madness. The purpose of marriage was to have

From *Everyday Life: Ancient Times* © 2006 Good Year Books.

children; love never entered the picture. Marriages were arranged; husbands were usually around thirty years of age and in most city-states brides were fourteen or fifteen. Girls, we are told, played with dolls right up to their wedding day, when they were expected to leave the dolls at the altar of Artemis, the goddess of unmarried girls.

Because the sole purpose of marriage was to have children, single people in Greece were frowned upon. Most city-states even had laws forbidding being single. Little was done, however, to enforce these measures. Except in Sparta. Sparta viewed bachelorhood as a serious offense and took steps to prod unmarried males to action. Military commanders would force bachelors to march naked through the marketplace. They were jeered at and sometimes even assaulted, and, because this event always took place in the dead of winter, it is safe to assume that they were also uncomfortable. History does not reveal the number of bachelors who consented to a trip to the altar because of this annual humiliation.

The Greeks were equally as stern with their children. Even in Athens, the most democratic of the city-states, a father had the right to reject a child shortly after birth if the family was too poor or had too many girls or the child was disabled. He had the right to leave the child in some public place to die. Matters were worse in Sparta, where weak or deformed babies were left on a mountainside to die of exposure. If, however, a child was accepted by the father, he or she led a carefree existence for the next six years.

In Rome, as in Greece, life centered around the father. In the early republic, the father or oldest male, in fact, held the power of life and death over his entire family. Any member who incurred his wrath could be killed or sold into slavery. Unwanted children were often abandoned to "the elements." Fortunately, such extreme action was seldom taken. In addition to the husband, the extended Roman family consisted of the wife, the children, married sons and their families, the grandparents, and all the slaves.

As in Greece, all Roman men were expected to marry and raise a family. Those who did not had to pay a bachelor tax. Marriages were often prearranged, sometimes when boys and girls were no more than infants. Girls were officially engaged when they were ten years old and married by their mid-teens. Their husbands were usually in their twenties.

The Roman groom presented his fiancée with an engagement ring, which he placed on the third finger of her left hand, the same finger on which people wear weddings rings today. The Romans believed that a nerve ran from the

Everyday Life: Ancient Times

ring finger directly to the heart. The ring was symbolic of the gentleman's pledge to honor his promise of marriage.

Once married, Roman wives were not confined to the home as were their Greek counterparts. They could go about freely, and many held jobs. They could even join their husbands in entertaining guests. But they lacked political rights; they could neither vote nor hold public office. Politics was a domain reserved exclusively for their husbands.

Sculpture of an Etruscan couple from the sixth century BC. The Etruscans were the rulers of early Rome.

During the years of the Roman republic, which extended from 509–27 BC, the family was a strong and close-knit unit. The father taught his sons obedience and good citizenship, while the mother taught her daughters how to cook, spin, and weave. Sometimes she even taught them to read, write, and do math. Family life changed sometime after the republic became the Roman Empire in 27 BC (The Western Roman Empire lasted until AD 476, while the Eastern Roman Empire, known as the Byzantine Empire, fell apart in 1453.) In the years when the Eastern Roman Empire was on the verge of collapse, family life broke down, and virtues once held dear disappeared.

If you are thinking that all ancient societies had similar views about marriage and the family, you will surely be surprised when you read about the Egyptians. It was in ancient Egypt that women enjoyed more rights and held a higher position than women in any other ancient civilization.

In Egypt, such a thing as courtship really existed, and likely as not it was the female who took the initiative. Many love letters written from women to men have survived the centuries. Here is an excerpt from a real letter that illustrates quite well how forward Egyptian women could be: "Oh my beautiful friend, my desire is to become, as thy wife, the mistress (manager or possessor) of all thy possessions."

Now that is about as blunt as one can put it! Such directness probably stemmed from the fact that women in Egypt could inherit and own property.

From *Everyday Life: Ancient Times* © 2006 Good Year Books.

Even though her husband might take over responsibility for any property she brought to the marriage, the wife still maintained its ownership. She could then pass on the property to her children. Furthermore, she could operate a business if she chose to do so. The rights granted to Egyptian women stunned visitors from outside Egypt. Greeks who visited the land of the Nile referred to Egyptian men as "henpecked."

Because women in Egypt were held in such high esteem, it naturally follows that children were also treated well. This was not the case in Mesopotamia, where many kingdoms rose and fell in a region that roughly corresponds to present-day Iraq. Parents in the Tigris and Euphrates valleys, where Mesopotamia lay, could disown their children and have them exiled to the countryside to fend for themselves.

The back of the throne of Tutankhamen depicting an Egyptian pharaoh and his wife. She is helping him get dressed.

Women in Mesopotamia enjoyed many of the same rights as those in Egypt. They could own property, open shops, and serve as priestesses in the temples. They fared less well, however, when it came to marriage. Their husbands could divorce them for the flimsiest of reasons or sell them to pay off debts. If accused and found guilty of infidelity, their punishment was quite severe. They were drowned.

In both ancient China and ancient India, girls were married very young. In India, they were no more than seven or eight years old when they were wed to men often four times their age. Still, they were treated quite well compared to women in China. In China, wives were subservient in all things. They did not eat with their husbands nor live in the same parts of the house. Their seclusion was shared in part by their children, who could only see their fathers once every ten days, and then only if they were on their best behavior.

You learned earlier about sickly babies in Sparta being abandoned to die. But the fate that befell some Chinese girl babies was even worse. Because their fathers considered girls a burden, they were sometimes left outside to die from the cold or to be eaten by the pigs!

Now that you've studied marriage and family life in ancient times, aren't you glad you were born a few thousand years later?

Name _____ Date _____

Research the Ancient World

How familiar are you with the ancient world? Can you go to a wall map and point out the locations of ancient Egypt and Mesopotamia? Can you locate Athens and Sparta or indicate the boundaries of the Roman Empire? Are you familiar with the types of government that ruled these ancient states and kingdoms?

Here are six questions concerning early civilizations and societies. You can find answers to them by consulting either your textbook, an encyclopedia, the Internet or any book dealing with the ancient world.

1. Early civilizations in Egypt, Mesopotamia, India, and China sprang up around four famous river valleys. These rivers and their locations are as follows:

    River(s)   **Location**

    _____   _____

    _____   _____

    _____   _____

    _____   _____

2. The word *Mesopotamia* means _____ _____ .

3. Many peoples and empires rose and fell in Mesopotamia in ancient times. Four of these were

    _____ , _____ ,

    _____ , and _____ .

4. The ancient Greeks never united to form one nation. Instead, they remained separated into city-states. A city-state is _____ _____ _____

5. Ancient Rome was a republic long before it became an empire. A republic is _____ _____ _____ .

6. Rome was an empire for some 500 years. An empire is defined as _____ _____ _____ .

From *Everyday Life: Ancient Times* © 2006 Good Year Books.

Name _____ Date _____

Recall Information You Have Read

How well do you recall information you have read? Without looking back over the chapter, test yourself by writing your best answers to four questions pertaining to ancient marriage and family life.

1. How did betrothals, or engagements, come about in most ancient societies?

_____

_____

_____

_____

2. Compare the status of women in Greece and Rome.

_____

_____

_____

_____

3. Explain how women in Ancient Egypt were far better off than their counterparts in other places.

_____

_____

_____

_____

_____

4. How were children looked upon and treated in Greece, Mesopotamia, and China? Compare their lot with children in such places as Rome and Egypt.

_____

_____

_____

_____

_____

Name _____ Date _____

Fill in a Venn Diagram

Fill in the Venn diagram to compare home life in ancient times with home life today. Write facts about each in the appropriate place. List characteristics common to both where the circles overlap.

Ancient Times

Both

Today

From Everyday Life: Ancient Times © 2006 Good Year Books.

Name _____ Date _____

Use Your Critical Thinking Skills

Think about the four questions posed on this page. Then write your best answer to each.

1. What might a young girl of ancient times have been thinking as she prepared to marry an older man she had yet to meet? Do you think she was happy? Frightened? Resigned to her fate? Explain your answer.

   _____

   _____

   _____

   _____

2. Why do you think many ancient societies passed laws forbidding bachelorhood? Were such laws fair? Why or why not?

   _____

   _____

   _____

   _____

3. List reasons why women in most ancient societies were regarded as second-class citizens.

   _____

   _____

   _____

   _____

4. Imagine yourself as a child in one of the ancient civilizations. What are some of the ways your life would be different?

   _____

   _____

   _____

   _____

CHAPTER 2

Housing

As is true of any time in history, the kinds of homes people occupied depended on their position and wealth. If rich and powerful, they might have lived in a palace or a country villa. If not-so-rich and powerful, they probably had to be content with a house made of sun-dried brick or even mud. In this chapter, you will get a glimpse at the homes of all classes.

Mud huts similar to the one shown in this model were home to Egypt's peasants. Such huts were small and offered few comforts.

In the sun-drenched land of ancient Egypt, the vast majority of people lived in mud huts. The typical hut had one room with no windows and one door. The roof and, sometimes, the walls were made of palm branches and straw that was covered with a coating of thick mud. Egyptian peasants were fortunate that Egypt receives very little rainfall; a good downpour might have brought the entire structure down on top of them.

Artisans fared better than the peasants. They lived in houses of unbaked brick. The usual pattern was three rooms, with the front room used for business and keeping animals. Some could even boast of two stories and a garden. Those who did have two stories had the advantage of sleeping on the roof, if they so desired. An outside stairway led directly to the top of the house. With the intense heat characteristic of the Nile region, Egyptians probably slept outside their houses more than inside (under the protection of mosquito nets, of course!).

Nobles and priests made up the Egyptian upper class and consequently lived in royal splendor. While the priests resided in temples, the nobles built magnificent villas of whitewashed, sun-dried brick. Some even had bathrooms fed by running water. Irrigation made it possible for a noble's villa to have a private courtyard garden and palm trees to shade the house from the searing sun. Houses usually had high, small windows to let out the heat.

In Mesopotamia to the northeast, mud turned into sun-dried brick was also the material used for construction. The typical peasant house was rectangular in shape and consisted of two or three rooms. It had an oven, a fireplace, and a chimney. Later, people began building round, domed houses.

From *Everyday Life: Ancient Times* © 2006 GoodYear Books.

The well-to-do of Mesopotamia lived in two-story brick houses that were whitewashed inside and out. Unlike the peasant's drab mud hut, the aristocrat's home was bright and cheery. It also contained more comforts. On the ground floor one would find a kitchen, a lavatory, a storeroom, a room for entertainment, and quarters for the servants. The family's living quarters were on the second floor. There, on hot summer nights, they mimicked the Egyptians by sleeping on the roof.

Although the Greeks to the east enjoyed a more moderate climate and therefore had no need to sleep on their roofs, their houses, for the most part, were also made of sun-dried brick. (A few were made of stone.) The brick in turn was covered with stucco, over which a coat of whitewash was applied. Because the brick crumbled easily, the houses were not very strong and needed regular repair. The inside of the house was as simple as the outside. Floors in poor homes were usually of hard dirt and covered with a straw mat. Richer men's houses had floors of flat or small round stones, sometimes with mosaics and imported rugs. Still, they were probably just as cold in the winter as those of dirt. Greek houses were unheated except for small pans of hot coals that burned in the center of a particular room. Usually, there was a room or rooms in the back where the women lived.

The weather in Greece is fairly comfortable nine months of every year, so people stayed outdoors much of the time. Houses were usually built around a courtyard, so women could be outside in the privacy of their homes. When the weather turned colder, the Greeks retired to rooms constructed to make use of the warmth and light of the sun. Light filtered into rooms that faced inward upon a courtyard, open to the air and sunshine. Thus, when people were home, they looked in and not out. Sometimes, in larger houses, there were two courtyards: one for the men and the boys and another for the ladies and the girls. While the men discussed politics and other matters, the women tended to such chores as weaving and supervised the daily activities of the household slaves.

Greek homes were sparsely furnished. There were beds, a few chairs, couches, chests, and some tables. That was about it. Of particular interest are the three-legged tables used for eating. Three legs gave more stability (a tripod is the most stable shape) on uneven floors. When the Greeks had to write something, they usually used their knees as tables.

Greek houses had bathrooms, with a basin and tub for washing. Some even had toilets looking very like modern ones and hooked up to drains. There were also public baths and public toilets.

Many houses had their own water tank or wells. Otherwise, to obtain water for drinking and bathing, slaves (or women too poor to have slaves) filled large clay jars at a fountain house located near the agora, or marketplace, and carried them home. Greek men, of course, never lent a hand in what was considered "woman's work."

The interior of a wealthy Roman's house, as envisioned by painter Luigi Bazzani in 1882.

Unlike the Greeks, wealthy Romans did have running water inside their homes, although poorer Romans had to get their water from public fountains. This was made possible by aqueducts that connected cities with mountain springs. Built of brick and stone, aqueducts were devices through which precious water flowed directly into homes and public baths from mountainous areas. In time, some two hundred cities throughout the Roman Empire were supplied with running water by aqueducts. Most Romans, however, did not have the luxury of running water.

Romans were not as sophisticated about disposing of their garbage. It was dumped in the street for street sweepers to clean up. There were laws against dumping your garbage on passersby, but that seems to have happened quite a bit.

Wealthier Romans lived in townhomes or country villas. Usually, there was a large reception room in front, called the *atrium*, where the father entertained his guests. An opening in the center of the room let in light, and a pool or basin underneath served to catch rainwater.

You have probably seen pictures depicting the country homes of wealthier Romans. Such villas usually had a garden and an open courtyard to the back of the house, complete with columns, fountains, and statues. Opening off the courtyard were even more rooms: extra bedrooms, gaming rooms, and rooms for books and art collections. There were even rooms for lounging, something aristocratic Romans apparently spent a lot of time doing.

The wealthiest Romans might also have a formal dining room called the *triclinium.* The word *triclinium* literally translates to mean "three couches." In this room, the noble Roman and his guests reclined on couches as they dined, bracing themselves on their left elbows as they ate with their right hands.

Rome's poor did not live in fancy villas and recline on couches. Instead, they packed themselves into large tenements (apartments) in the cities. These tenements were often six- or seven-story buildings of shoddy construction. Sometimes they collapsed, killing hundreds of occupants. Although Roman law tried to limit the height of tenements to some 70 feet, the rear of each building was often higher. One writer wrote of a man who had to ascend two hundred steps to reach his attic apartment! Residents either had to share a common kitchen or take their food to a baker to be cooked!

Whereas Roman and Greek cities were notoriously dirty, Mohenjo-Daro and Harappa, two large cities of ancient India (now southern Pakistan), were amazingly clean. Each city could boast of an advanced sanitation system and even houses that had rubbish chutes for disposing of garbage. Large, sturdy, two-story homes of baked brick lined the streets, and most had indoor baths and toilets that drained into underground sewers. Sometime around 1700 BC, however, both Mohenjo-Daro and Harappa disappeared, and the Indian civilization that followed was much less advanced. After that date, most people lived in simple mud houses of two or three rooms. None had indoor plumbing like earlier Indian homes.

In ancient China, most homes were made of wood. This was true regardless of the owner's social status. Nearly all, however, had the graceful, upward-turned eaves for which Chinese architecture is noted. One reason for the curved eaves was the Chinese belief that evil spirits only traveled in straight lines. With the eaves curved upward, such spirits supposedly just bounced off.

The homes of the rich in China were, of course, much larger than those of the poor. And they were filled with priceless possessions made of ceramics, glass, metal, and lacquer. In contrast, the home of the Chinese peasant consisted of a one-room structure with a dirt floor. (Sometimes he lived in a simple pit dug into the ground!) Sharing this humble abode with each family were their chickens, pigs, and dogs. Of all ancient peoples, the life of the Chinese peasant might have been the worst.

Name _____ Date _____

Make a Shoe Box Diorama

Make a shoe box diorama depicting a scene from everyday life in one of the homes described in the chapter. You may create either a replica of the house itself or a scene of its inhabitants going about their daily activities. A few possibilities might be:

1. a wealthy Roman family reclining on couches as they dine

2. a Chinese peasant family at home in their one-room abode with their pets and livestock

3. furnishings inside the typical Greek home

4. an Egyptian family sleeping on the roof of their brick home

5. a scene from an apartment in a Roman tenement

Or you may want to think of a scene to create.

Some of the materials you will need to make your diorama are:

1. A large shoe box

2. Construction paper

3. Markers or watercolors and paintbrush

4. Felt-tipped pen

5. Glue

6. Scissors

7. Modeling clay or small figurines of people and animals

From *Everyday Life: Ancient Times* © 2006 Good Year Books.

Name _____ Date _____

Use Context Clues to Complete Sentences

Fill in the blanks in the sentences using the words from the word box.

accommodate
apartments
better
contained
dug
feel
limited
little
luxury
measured
modern
offset
plight
quite
sparsely
supported

So you think your room at home is small and cramped? Do you wish you had more space to _____ all your things and your 140-pound Irish wolfhound? Do you _____ that life is treating you unfairly?

In spite of your _____, you would not get any sympathy from the common people of ancient Egypt. Suppose your entire house _____ only 8 feet by 10 feet! Try squeezing your 140-pound Irish wolfhound into that _____ space, along with your parents and three or four brothers and sisters!

Matters were a _____ better in Mesopotamia, where the typical peasant house _____ three rooms. Still, houses were _____ small compared to _____ homes. They did have an oven, a fireplace, and a chimney, but these amenities were not enough to _____ their drabness and lack of comfort.

Now suppose that you were a member of a poor, farming family in Ancient China. You might not even have the _____ of living in a real house. As you read in the chapter, some Chinese peasants lived in pits _____ into the ground. These pit houses had thatched roofs _____ by wooden or bamboo poles. Throw in a pig or two and a bunch of chickens and you can see these homes were far from being penthouse _____.

Although the Greeks and Romans had it considerably _____, their homes were still small and _____ furnished compared to ours today. So, stop complaining and count your blessings. And tell your Irish wolfhound to be a little more appreciative too!

Name _____ Date _____

Distinguish between Sentences and Fragments

Can you distinguish between a complete sentence and a fragment? Fragments are statements that either lack a verb or a subject or do not express a complete thought. Fragments may be used in certain situations, but it is usually best to use complete sentences when writing.

Following are a group of statements relating to chapter 2. Some are fragments, while others are complete sentences. On the line to the left of each, write F if the statement is a fragment or S if it is a sentence. In the space below each statement that you mark as a fragment, rewrite the statement to make it a complete sentence.

1. _____ Mud houses as far as the eye could see.

_____

2. _____ Ancient Egyptians sleeping on their roofs.

_____

3. _____ Egyptian nobles built magnificent homes of sun-dried brick.

_____

4. _____ Whereas most Mesopotamians lived in simple mud huts.

_____

5. _____ Greek homes contained little furniture.

_____

6. _____ Seated in their private courtyards, Greek men often passed the time discussing politics.

_____

7. _____ Wealthy Romans enjoyed the luxury of running water in their homes.

_____

8. _____ Romans dining while reclining on couches.

_____

9. _____ Chinese pithouses dug into the ground.

_____

From *Everyday Life: Ancient Times* © 2006 Good Year Books.

Name _____   Date _____

Solve Some Ancient Housing Word Problems

After reviewing such terms as *area*, *perimeter*, and *square feet*, solve these word problems and write their answers on the appropriate blank lines. Space is provided for you to work each problem.

1. The perimeter of Roman magistrate Marcus Cato's bedroom is 52 feet. His gaming room is an 11-by-13-foot rectangle. Which has the greater perimeter, his bedroom or his gaming room?

    His _____ has the greater perimeter.

2. Heracles, a wealthy Greek aristocrat, owns a large house in the country outside of Athens. Spacious rooms surround a courtyard that measures 30 feet by 50 feet. What is the area of Heracles' courtyard?

    The area is _____.

3. Arnak, a Mesopotamian peasant, is the proud owner of a three-room house. One room measures 10 feet by 12 feet, another 8 feet by 10 feet, and a third 11 feet by 13 feet. What is the total square footage of Arnak's house?

    The total square footage is _____.

Clothing and Appearance

If a group of people from ancient times were to suddenly appear in today's world, we can imagine their shock at the scene around them. Skyscrapers, suspension bridges, and superhighways would render them speechless and awestruck. Computers, VCRs, and television sets would leave them dumbfounded. And they would quickly scurry for cover at first sight of a speeding automobile or a supersonic jet airplane.

But what about our modern dress, especially that of a few of our students and others? Do you think our ancient visitors would be surprised at what they saw? Maybe not. They probably wouldn't see anything unusual about pierced ears (and other body parts) and purple hair! After all, in ancient times, many people pierced their ears and colored their hair. They also dyed the palms of their hands and the soles of their feet! Bet you don't know anyone who does that!

An Egyptian lady's cosmetic spoon, one of a number of items she kept in a special box.

No people were more into appearance than the ancient Egyptians. In addition to painting their palms and the soles of their feet, they colored around their eyes with eye paint that was either green (malachite) or dark gray (kohl) in color. This paint may have protected their eyes from the glare of the sun. They also painted their lips with red ochre mixed with oil or fat.

As if painting parts of the body were not enough, ancient Egyptians of both sexes covered their necks, chests, arms, wrists, and ankles with jewelry. They also daubed themselves liberally with perfumes, and many shaved their heads and wore wigs. Egyptian women started what must have been the most novel use of perfume in history. Pictures show them at banquets with what closely resembles huge jellyfish sitting atop their heads. These were actually cones of perfumed wax. As the evening wore on, the cones slowly melted and ran down the faces and shoulders of the ladies who wore them. Although we today might see the end result as a sticky mess, the Egyptians considered it fragrant and cooling.

In general, most Egyptians dressed in loose, white linen kilts or dresses, which helped them keep cool in the hot climate. Workers often wore only a brief loincloth as they labored in the heat. Children of both sexes went around

From Everyday Life: Ancient Times © 2006 GoodYear Books.

completely unclad until their teens, although girls did wear a string of beads around their waist. Both girls and boys wore earrings and necklaces and shaved their heads, leaving only something similar to a scalp lock on one side. A scalp lock is a long lock or tuft of hair hanging down one side of an otherwise shaved head.

Except for the Sumerians, the many different peoples who lived in Mesopotamia dressed in pretty much the same way. Whether Babylonian, Assyrian, Chaldean, or some other group, they wore long, colorful robes that reached to the feet. Both men and women wore their hair in long curls and bedecked themselves with numerous ornaments and rings. They also drenched themselves in perfume, just as the Egyptians did. Unlike the Egyptians, however, many of the men wore beards. Men in some parts of the region also were the first to wear trousers. The Middle Eastern custom of women wearing veils began among the Assyrians.

As for the Sumerians, these first occupants of the Tigris and Euphrates valleys wore a flounced, or pleated, garment of flax (linen) and wool. Women draped the garment from the left shoulder, while the men tied it at the waist and left the chest bare, giving them the appearance of wearing a kilt. Some men grew beards, but many were clean-shaven. For their part, Sumerian women were as much into ornaments as were the ladies of Egypt. Both men and women adorned themselves with earrings, necklaces, and bracelets. While most went barefoot or wore sandals, the more well-to-do sported shoes of soft leather that laced up the front.

Although in comparison the Greeks appear to have dressed simply, they too had a penchant for jewelry, ornaments, perfumes, and the like. Both men and women pinned their clothing with brooches. Every man wore at least one ring, and some women displayed jewelry on every finger. Women also flaunted bracelets, necklaces, earrings, good-luck charms, lockets, chains, and diadems (crowns). Lest you think the Greek female was pretentious about her appearance, consider the vanity of the well-to-do Greek male. Each morning, he hurried to his barber to have his hair braided and curled! Often he wore a headband around it. Only slaves had short hair. This practice continued until the latter days of the city-states, after which gentlemen kept their hair cropped short.

The chief garment of Greek ladies was the peplos, a long robe that fell to the ankles. Men wore a chiton, or belted tunic, that extended to the knees. Both sexes often wore a light cloak, called a *himation,* when they went out.

Men also sometimes wore what was called a *chlamys*, a short cape. Even outdoors people often went barefoot. When they did don footwear, both sexes usually wore sandals.

Statues and drawings seem to indicate that cleanliness was a top priority among ancient Greeks. However, because water was often scarce, only the rich could bathe daily. Between baths, average citizens "bathed" themselves with olive oil, which was rubbed all over the body and scraped off with a device called a *strigil*. Do you think such a practice was effective in bringing about good hygiene?

Statue of a woman shown wearing a peplos, the traditional garment worn by Greek women.

Thanks to the construction of the aqueducts, a similar shortage of water did not exist in ancient Rome. Rome, in fact, had some 900 public baths where, for a nominal fee equal to less than a penny, any citizen could spend part of a day bathing, exercising, reading, and catching up on the latest gossip. Although most emperors allowed mixed bathing, women usually frequented the baths in the morning hours and men in the evening. (You will learn more about the public baths of Rome in a later chapter.)

Once a Roman emerged spic-and-span from either a public bath or a private tub at home, he or she slipped into an outfit similar in style to that of the Greeks. Men wore a tunic while women donned a kind of dress called a *stola*. A stola was a high-waisted garment that reached to the ankle and was fastened at the shoulders with clasps. Although it was usually white or gray, it could also be bought in a variety of colors for a price.

While outdoors, men covered their tunic with a toga, a loose, draped wrap that was as wide as a man and three times as long, so it probably took some practice to master. The long piece of cloth was first arranged over the left shoulder. Then it was wrapped around the back, under the right arm, tucked into the belt, and then swung over the left shoulder again. (Don't try this at home with a sheet—you might not be able to untangle yourself!)

From *Everyday Life: Ancient Times* © 2006 Good Year Books.

When the Roman lady went out, she covered her stola with a brightly colored shawl called a *palla*. On her feet she wore either white, green, or yellow shoes. If she was truly fashionable, she probably wore a wig made from the hair of slave girls. If not, she might have dyed her hair blonde or powdered it with gold dust.

Instead of shoes, Roman men wore sandals. Those of the patrician, or upper, class wore sandals dyed red. Senators wore brown, while consuls, who were high government officials, went about in white. Many Roman men also wore wigs, some to hide their baldness and others to hide their true identities.

In ancient India, dress depended on one's caste. A caste is a rigid social class into which one is born and remains throughout life. The top group of castes consisted of the Brahmans, or priests, who dressed in simple cotton. Next came the warrior castes, which went about in colorful, baggy trousers, complemented by boots, a tunic, and a turban. Below the warriors were the merchants and the laborers, whose dress was nearly as simple as that of the priests. Men wore a dhoti, which in some ways resembled the Roman toga. Women dressed in the sari, a long piece of cloth that was wrapped around the body to form a kind of dress, with the loose end thrown over the head.

At the bottom of the Indian social order were the outcasts, or untouchables (see chapter 6). They included slaves and beggars who were reduced to wearing rags. Often they wore no clothing at all. They were joined in their naked state by Indian children, who, except for beads and rings, played and attended school in the buff.

No one in ancient China went around without clothes, probably because the weather was too cold. Except for the material used, all Chinese wore basically the same outfit. Men, women, and children dressed in a long tunic held in place by a belt or sash and topped off by a short jacket. Only the rich wore silk; poorer people made do with wool or cotton. A man's tunic had very long sleeves that served as pockets. Thus, he never "pocketed" anything; he "sleeved" it. Among the peasants, both men and women wore trousers beneath their tunics. This was because country women did the same kind of work as country men. They also wore shoes of straw. In the cities, women covered their trousers with skirts.

Chinese clothing was made to last and was passed down through several generations. Some people might wear clothing that was 80 or 90 years old! Do you think such "hand-me-downs" were ever a source of complaint among Chinese youngsters?

Name _____   Date _____

Solve a Clothing Puzzle

ACROSS

2 Member of Roman upper class
7 Outcastes of India
11 Dress worn by Indian women
13 Instrument used to scrape oil from the body
14 Shawl worn by Roman women
15 Long robe worn by Greek women

DOWN

1 Light cloak worn by Greek men
3 Government official in Rome
4 Used by Egyptians to color their eyes
5 Device that brought water from mountain streams
6 Garment worn by most Indian men
8 Long piece of cloth worn by Roman men
9 A priest of India
10 A crown
11 Dress worn by Roman women
12 Tunic worn by Greek men

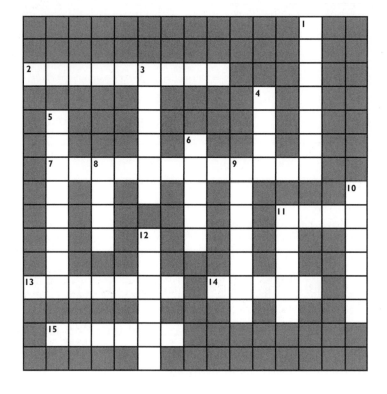

From *Everyday Life: Ancient Times* © 2006 Good Year Books.

Name _____ Date _____

Write a Time Travel Dialogue

Imagine yourself whisked back to Roman times in the midst of a party hosted by an important Roman aristocrat. The men present are decked out in impressive togas, while the women are dressed in their best stolas. For your part, you are wearing frayed shorts, a T-shirt with "Middle School Students Are Cool!" inscribed on the front, and tennis shoes that have seen better days.

With this scenario in mind, create a dialogue that might take place between yourself and the stunned Romans.

CHAPTER 4

Food and Drink

S uppose that after time-traveling back to ancient Rome and finding yourself at the banquet described in the final activity for chapter 3, you are urged to stay for dinner. Curious, you accept the invitation. After being tortured for years with broccoli and the like by your parents, you are naturally interested in seeing if the Romans served anything better.

You recline on a couch between two Roman guests and closely observe what has been set out on the table before you. Soon you wish you had declined the invitation and climbed back into your time machine. These are the years of the empire—years when the Romans have forsaken their simple diet for one that is exotic and quite weird. In the center of the table is a small bowl of snail snacks, fried in oil and served piping hot. Nearby is a plate of stuffed dormice (yes, mice!), which you soon learn is a prized delicacy. But wait! You haven't seen anything yet! As your eyes further survey the table, they come to rest on the main dish: boiled ostrich.

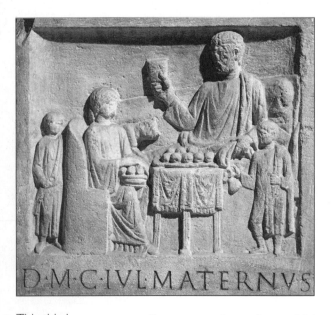

This third-century AD stone-relief shows a Roman family enjoying a meal together.

We will revisit the Romans later. First, however, we shall return to Ancient Egypt, where people did not eat dormice and ostriches. They also did not eat flamingo tongues or rose pie, the ingredients of which included, in addition to rose petals and other things, four cooked calves' brains!

In comparison, it could be argued that what the Egyptians ate was bland and boring. Most people subsisted on a diet of bread and on such vegetables as lettuce, onions, garlic, beans, and lentils. On special holidays, they might also treat themselves to fruit. Such fruit included figs, dates, grapes, and pomegranates. The only strange thing associated with Egyptian food was that, in making bread, they kneaded the dough with their feet!

Common people in Egypt augmented their diet with fresh and dried fish, which they caught in fishing nets or wicker traps; wealthier fisherman could afford harpoons. Of course, anyone fishing in the Nile had to keep their eyes peeled for hungry crocodiles hunting them! The average person ate meat only on special occasions because there was not enough land to keep large livestock herds.

While peasants and other commoners made do with simple fare, members of the Egyptian nobility gorged themselves on all sorts of fruits and meats. Among the latter, they ate beef, veal, antelope, gazelle, and various kinds of wild fowl. Unlike the lower classes who drank barley beer, the nobles washed down their meals with wine.

In Mesopotamia, people ate many of the same things as the Egyptians. Wheat and barley were staple crops, as was flax, used for clothing and oil. Farmers also grew a variety of vegetables. These included eggplant, cucumbers, garlic, onions, lentils, lettuce, beets, turnips, and radishes. Dates and figs were common fruits. Sesame, a herb used to flavor bread and other foods, was also cultivated. The Mesopotamians made beer from corn, and they produced wine from dates. They also were among the first to grow grapes and olives.

Although the Sumerians seem to have eaten goats and sheep (from whose milk they also made cheese and butter) as well as cattle, doves, chickens, ducks, and fish, many peoples of Mesopotamia apparently ate a largely vegetarian diet. They ate fish, but other meats were usually reserved for the aristocracy. Even the mighty Assyrian army, which was always making life extremely uncomfortable for any unfortunate people they conquered, got by mainly on vegetarian rations.

One example of the culinary excesses of the aristocracy of Mesopotamia is Ashurnasirpal II, an Assyrian king who ruled in the ninth century BC Ashurnasirpal II built a magnificent palace on the Tigris River at Calah, where he held court in grand style. He was known to have hosted a banquet for nearly seventy thousand people that lasted ten days to celebrate the rebuilding of Calah. At one such feast, guests ate more than two thousand oxen and sixteen thousand sheep. Apparently still having room for more, they also consumed countless numbers of game birds. The kegs of wine they downed at this one banquet must have set a record.

By contrast, what the Greeks ate and drank was extremely moderate. This was due both to their lifestyle and their arid land. Only about a fourth of Greek land is suitable for farming; the rest is mountainous. In ancient times, the people grew mainly grain, grapes, and olives. Olives distinguished Greek farming; the Greeks used them to make a spread for their bread, oil for cleaning their bodies, and fuel for their lamps.

Even though we read mostly about Greek philosophers and poets, farming was the basis of Greek society, and most Greeks had small farms. In most of the ancient world, farmers were poor peasants who had to turn over their crops to

wealthy nobles, who gave them meager rations. Not so in Greece, where farmers were independent and free to sell their crops in the markets.

On the small amount of land suitable for farming, the Greeks also grew many of the same fruits and vegetables found in Egypt and Mesopotamia: lentils, figs, beans, peas, lettuce, cabbage, onions, and garlic. Some of these formed the basis of a mid-morning meal, one of two meals eaten daily by most Greeks. At sunset, a second meal was taken and usually consisted of bread, cheese, olives, figs, and maybe some fish. Most Greeks ate very little meat; sheep were raised for wool and goats for cheese. With their meals, the Greeks drank a mixture of wine and water. Milk was thought fit only for animals and barbarians, although it was used for making cheese and for medicinal purposes. People ate while reclining on couches.

Greek servants preparing a meal. This scene is from an Early Corinthian vase, dating to about 600 BC.

Most Greeks throughout the various city-states ate the same kinds of foods. Not so, however, in Sparta. Sparta was a military state where its citizens were expected to endure all manner of hardships, not the least of which was a sparse diet. Men, who served in the army from age of twenty to sixty and who actually began training at age seven, were required to eat at a common mess. Even ordinary citizens had to eat one meal a day at a public dining facility. Such a meal normally consisted of bread and wine, a portion of which had to be provided by the diners themselves. There was never enough to fill the stomach, the idea being that a hungry Spartan was a tough Spartan.

At the beginning of the chapter, you were introduced to the eating habits of some Romans. Suffice it to say that most people throughout the Roman Empire did not eat dormice and ostriches, nor did they gorge themselves to the point of nausea. Common citizens dined mostly on what they had eaten during the days of the republic. Meals consisted generally of olives, grapes, honey, vegetable stews, and foods made from wheat: breads, porridge, and pancakes. On special occasions, such as holidays and weddings, pork and mutton might have been added to a meal. Wealthier Romans ate a three-course dinner, the main meal of the day, with hors d'oeuvres, a meat course, and fruit dessert.

From *Everyday Life: Ancient Times* © 2006 Good Year Books.

In the latter days of Rome, the rich seemed determined to eat themselves into decline. For banquets, the usual three courses expanded to six or more. In addition to such fare as ostrich and dormouse, a fancy banquet might include lobster, eel, chicken, roast pig, boar, venison, goat, lamb, flamingo, and rabbit. One course alone might consist of eggs, sardines, oysters, honey, mushrooms, radishes, and salads. Before these were eaten, however, guests warmed up on such appetizers as boiled tree fungi with peppered fish-fat sauce and sow's udders stuffed with salted sea urchins. (No kidding!) At the end, there was always dessert. Besides rose pie, guests had their choice of a variety of cakes, fruits, and nuts.

It goes without saying that what the Chinese and Indians ate paled in comparison to their ancient neighbors. But they did have their moments. In China, feasts were rare, but when they did occur in the homes of the wealthy, no expense was spared to satisfy the tastes of the invited guests. How about snails, dog meat, turtles, and raw meat topped with ant eggs as the main part of the meal? Or maybe dainty dishes prepared from the likes of grubs, silkworms, fish intestines, rats, and water-snakes.

Ancient Chinese peasants grew many of the same vegetables pictured here, in this scene from a present-day market.

The common people of ancient China got by on such fare as rice, wheat noodles, bean curd, turnips, and melons. Depending on the area, they might also enjoy oranges, tangerines, bananas, and coconuts. In the absence of meat, many ate stewed frogs.

What people ate in ancient India depended on their caste, or class. The Hindu ideal was to be vegetarian, except for dairy products, in order not to harm any animals. Brahmans were expected to follow this diet. Members of the warrior caste might eat eggs and certain meats, though, to promote aggression. Some people in lower castes ate pork or chicken, meats that were considered unclean. No Hindus ate cows, which were sacred. Hungry, anyone?

Name _____ Date _____

Make False Statements True

All of the statements on this page are false. Change the words in italics to make them true. Write the replacement words on the lines following the statements.

1. The *Egyptians* ate while reclining on couches. _____

2. Ordinary citizens in *Athens* had to eat one meal a day in a communal dining hall. _____

3. Boiled ostrich was a favorite dish of wealthy *Mesopotamians*. _____

4. The *Greeks* used their feet to knead dough for their bread. _____

5. Drinking wine was restricted to nobles in *China*. _____

6. Ashurnasirpal II was a king of *Egypt*. _____

7. In *China*, what people ate depended on the caste to which they belonged. _____

8. The common people of Egypt drank *wine* with their meals. _____

9. Roughly *one-half* of the land in Greece is suitable for farming. _____

10. *Rutabagas* distinguished Greek agriculture. _____

11. Most ancient Greeks ate *three* meals a day. _____

12. The Greeks never drank *water*, considering it fit only for animals and barbarians. _____

13. Spartan men were required to serve in the army from age twenty to *forty*. _____

14. If one desired boiled tree fungi with peppered fish-fat sauce or sow's udders stuffed with salted sea urchins, he or she would seek out the table of an ancient *Egyptian*. _____

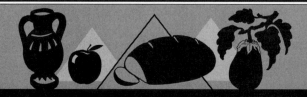

Name _____ Date _____

Write a Letter

Imagine you are living in Roman times and have just attended a banquet at the home of a wealthy patrician named Marcus Marcellus. You were impressed by the food served and you thoroughly enjoyed the entertainment your host provided in the form of musicians, dancers, and acrobats.

Using your best grammar and sentence structure, write a letter to your host expressing your appreciation for an evening well spent.

March 20, AD 214

Dear Marcus Marcellus,

_____

_____

_____

_____

_____

_____

_____

_____

_____

_____

_____

_____

_____

_____

_____

_____

_____

_____

Sincerely,

_____

(Your Name)

Name _____ Date _____

Make a Food Mobile

You learned in chapter 4 that ancient peoples ate and enjoyed different kinds of food. They also had access to many of the foods that we eat today. With a few simple materials, you can make a mobile depicting some of the favorite dishes of each of the ancient civilizations covered in the chapter.

To make a more detailed mobile, cut pieces of stiff wire in lengths of about 6 inches. Slightly bend each piece in the middle to give it a rainbow shape. Attach a card to each end of the wire strip. Tie different lengths of string to the middle of the pieces of wire and then hang the strips from the bottom of the clothes hanger.

Here Is What You Will Need:

1. Large clothes hanger
2. Construction paper or small index cards
3. Crayons or coloring pencils
4. Felt-tipped pen
5. Hole punch
6. String
7. Some stiff wire (optional)

Here Is What You Do:

1. On pieces of construction paper or index cards cut to a size of 2 inches by 3 inches (or a little larger if you like), write in large letters the names of the various civilizations mentioned in chapter 4: Egypt, Mesopotamia, Greece, and so on.

2. On the back of each card, list some of the favorite foods of the civilization whose name appears on the front.

3. Punch a hole at the top of each card.

4. Insert and tie a piece of string through the hole at the top of each card. Make your pieces of string different lengths so you can stagger your cards on the clothes hanger.

5. Attach the cards to the bottom of the clothes hanger.

6. Make a sign reading "Food in Ancient Times" and attach it to the top of the hanger.

From *Everyday Life: Ancient Times* © 2006 Good Year Books.

Name _____   Date _____

Search Out Some Food Facts

Turning our attention from the past to the present, consult an encyclopedia or other source and explain how what people eat and the manner in which they eat it are in part determined by the following factors:

Geography

_____

_____

_____

_____

Religion

_____

_____

_____

_____

Customs

_____

_____

_____

_____

Economy

_____

_____

_____

Fads and Advertisements

_____

_____

_____

_____

Fun and Amusements

ost people in ancient times were too busy trying to eke out a living to devote much attention to entertainment. But, as you will learn on the following pages, even the lower classes enjoyed moments of fun and recreation. In some places huge games were held that were free to the public. In Rome, for example, even the poorest citizen could betake himself to a coliseum or racetrack and cheer for his favorite gladiator or charioteer. In Greece, he could attend the Olympic Games or in Assyria he could clamber to the top of a hillside and watch his king hunt lions on his private preserve. More will be said about these public spectacles (and others) later in the chapter.

An Egyptian nobleman hunting waterfowl with his wife and daughter. His daughter is pictured holding onto her father's leg.

What we know about amusements in ancient Egypt comes primarily from two sources: wall paintings discovered in royal tombs and the writings of the Greek historian Herodotus. Herodotus, who is known as the Father of History, visited Egypt in the fifth century BC and took notes on everything he saw. His observations of the Egyptian nobility at play provide us with interesting little details that mere wall paintings cannot convey.

Herodotus, for example, writes that at the conclusion of a raucous banquet, the host performed a ritual that was strange, to say the least. Shortly before the guests left, one of the household slaves walked about the house displaying a small coffin containing a wooden likeness of the host himself. The purpose of this act was to remind those in attendance of their mortality. Considering they had probably just washed down huge amounts of raw fish and raw fowl with equally huge quantities of alcohol, their mortality at the moment might not have been foremost in their minds.

Egyptians of all classes enjoyed fowling. The rich viewed such an activity as sport, but to commoners it was a means of earning a living. Although the nobles sometimes felled ducks and other birds with a boomerang, a large net was generally used to entrap water fowl. The net was closed by means of a rope pulled by several Egyptians concealed in the bushes. The signal to pull the rope

From *Everyday Life: Ancient Times* © 2006 GoodYear Books.

was given by a lookout who wore a cap shaped like a duck. Apparently this simple disguise was enough to lull the unsuspecting birds into a false sense of security.

Egyptians also enjoyed wrestling, bare-fisted boxing, and swimming. (Considering that parts of the Nile River are infested with crocodiles and hippopotamuses, the latter might have been a hazardous activity.) A popular spectator sport involved watching a rousing water tournament in which two boat teams armed with long poles attempted to knock each other into the water. Finally, Egyptians took delight in picnics and various board games. The most popular of the latter was senet, a strategy game, as well as a game that resembled checkers.

Children in ancient Egypt played games and had toys similar to those of children today. They engaged in wrestling, leapfrog, and racing and enjoyed such toys as tops, dolls, balls, and marbles. Archaeologists have also unearthed toy animals whose mouths opened or whose tails moved with the pull of a string.

Herodotus also visited Mesopotamia, where he wrote about children playing games that mimicked adult life. One of his stories concerned the future Persian king Cyrus II at age ten playing a game called "Kings" with his friends. Because the others always selected him as king, Cyrus enjoyed the privilege of punishing any of his "subjects" who disobeyed him. Herodotus wrote that one boy who refused to obey Cyrus was firmly held by the others while the future king flogged him soundly with a whip.

Much adult entertainment in Mesopotamia took place in public squares. Scenes on clay tablets and bas-reliefs (carvings in which the figures stand out slightly from the background) show wrestlers and bare-fisted boxers in the heat of competition. Other scenes depict people playing games of chance with dice, as well as storytellers and musicians performing for audiences.

When it came to having fun, few ancient people could top the Greeks. *Male* Greeks, that is. As you learned in chapter 1, Greek women, for the most part, were confined to their homes. They were expected to tend to "wifely" duties and only ventured out with their husbands' permission.

Greek men, on the other hand, were free to enjoy many activities and amusements. Because every town and city had outside gymnasiums and theaters, there was always something to do or see. Both men and boys enjoyed foot races and wrestling, and many played games similar to hockey and rugby. They also relished gathering at a hillside theater and watching the latest tragedy or comedy.

The most popular entertainment event in ancient Greece was the Olympic Games. A truce was always called before the games so that free-born Greeks from all the city-states (which were often fighting with each other) could travel to the games. Held every four years on the plains of Olympia, the games attracted contestants from all the city-states. For up to five grueling days, young men competed in a variety of games—including running, wrestling, and boxing—hoping for victory and glory. The olive wreath they received for winning were just as important to the victors as medals are to today's champions.

Entrance to the stadium at Olympia, Greece. Olympia was the site of the first Olympic Games, held in 776 BC.

One of the premier events at the Olympic Games was the pentathlon. This was actually five contests in one. Each athlete raced, jumped, wrestled, threw the discus, and hurled the javelin. In addition to the regular wrestling in the pentathlon, there was another event call the *pankration*, a mix of boxing and wrestling. Talk about a sock-it-to-'em sport! A contestant was permitted to strangle, kick, or break the fingers of his opponent. He could even jump up and down on his opponent's stomach! In effect, nothing was barred except biting and gouging out the eyes.

The more glamorous events were the equestrian events. An interesting feature of these events was that the owner of the horses was declared the winner—even if he didn't compete in the race. Thus, in later days, women could win these events, even though they were not allowed to attend the games. The wildest equestrian event was the four-horse chariot race, where drivers raced twelve times around an oval track, called a *hippodrome*, covering a distance of about nine miles. Chariot racing was a dangerous sport. In one forty chariot race, only one driver finished the race. Imagine 160 horses vying for position on one track. Talk about thrills, chills, and spills!

The Romans also had chariot races. These were not part of the Olympic Games but were instead held regularly at giant arenas called *circuses*. The largest and most popular was the Circus Maximus in Rome, which could accommodate more than 250,000 screaming spectators. Gambling at these races was heavy, and fortunes were won and lost in record time. Mishaps were

From *Everyday Life: Ancient Times* © 2006 Good Year Books.

many, as aggressive driving on the part of charioteers was expected and encouraged. Drivers purposely bumped each other, cut each other off, and ran over any driver who overturned. Bodies, chariots, and horses sometimes became entangled in a massive pile on the track. And the fans in attendance cheered themselves hoarse!

The violence associated with Roman chariot races reveals the character of Roman entertainment in the empire's latter days. People packed the Colosseum in Rome and other amphitheaters to watch all manner of gruesome contests. Sometimes gladiators fought; at other times men were pitted against wild animals, or condemned prisoners were executed. Popular history tells of early Christians being thrown to the lions, but it's not clear how often this really happened. There were even times when the Colosseum was flooded with water to accommodate sham naval battles. In the latter contests, boatloads of prisoners and criminals hacked and fought each other to the death. History records that even the ladies in attendance screamed with delight.

Roman children imitated their elders in play. Pictures reveal small boys playing charioteer in carts pulled by dogs, sheep, and goats. Even toddlers got into the act, harnessing mice to tiny carts and urging them to race! Small wonder that when these lads grew up they quickly beat a path to the nearest circus.

While not attending an event at an amphitheater or circus, a Roman might seek entertainment at a public bath. The largest public bath in the empire was built by the Emperor Caracella in the third century AD. It covered some 28 acres and could accommodate sixteen hundred bathers a day. At this and other baths, Romans, in addition to bathing, could engage in calisthenics, listen to lectures and musical performances, or simply lounge around and gossip. Even wealthy Romans who had their own facilities at home sought out the public baths as places of entertainment and relaxation.

As for the Chinese, they were obsessed with games of chance and strategy. They invented chess, dominoes, playing cards, and backgammon, and they often gambled themselves into debt at each. They also invented polo and played a game similar to football, using a ball made from the bladder of an animal.

In India, the common people partially passed the time dancing and listening to music. They too seemed addicted to gambling at games of chance. Indian children played with toy animals whose heads bobbed up and down and with miniature ox carts pulled by a string. Archaeologists have also unearthed whistles and other playthings made of terra cotta, or baked clay.

Name _____ Date _____

Write a Lead Paragraph for *The Roman Times*

Newspapers did not exist in Roman times. Although some sources trace the history of the newspaper back to Rome and Julius Caesar, what Caesar published were one-page announcements that were posted throughout the city. They were in no way real newspapers.

Suppose, however, that newspapers did exist in those days and that you are a roving reporter for *The Roman Times* who has been assigned to cover a chariot race at the Circus Maximus. With this in mind, write the lead, or first, paragraph of a story about the race that would go along with the headline provided for you. Be sure to include answers to the five "W" questions (Who? What? When? Where? and Why?) that are characteristic of a good lead paragraph. Continue on the back of the page if necessary.

The Roman Times

★ ★ ★ ★ ★ April 3, AD 214 ★ ★ ★ ★ ★

Fearless Fabius Wins Again!

Nips Bad Brutus by a Nose

_____
_____
_____
_____
_____
_____
_____
_____
_____
_____
_____
_____
_____
_____
_____
_____
_____
_____

From *Everyday Life: Ancient Times* © 2006 Good Year Books.

Name _____ Date _____

Evaluate Leisure Activities

Leisure activities were just as important to people in ancient times as they are today. People throughout history, in fact, have always treasured every minute they could find for fun and amusement.

On the lines provided, write a paper explaining why recreation and entertainment are so important to all of us.

_____

_____

_____

_____

_____

_____

_____

_____

_____

_____

_____

_____

_____

_____

_____

_____

_____

_____

_____

_____

_____

_____

_____

Name _____ Date _____

Fill in a Venn Diagram

Fill in the Venn diagram to compare what people did for fun and amusement in ancient times with what people do today. Write facts about each in the appropriate place. List characteristics common to both where the circles overlap.

Ancient Times

Both

Today

From Everyday Life: Ancient Times © 2006 Good Year Books.

Name _____ Date _____

Correct Erroneous Petronius's Math

Erroneous Petronius is a Roman schoolboy who is not very good at math. Try as he might, he always comes up with the wrong answers.

Opposite are four word problems dealing with the Circus Maximus in Rome. Each contains an answer arrived at by Erroneous, which, of course, is incorrect. In the space provided, work each problem and write the correct answer on the appropriate line. In doing so, you will provide an invaluable service to Erroneous.

1. The Circus Maximus measures 680 yards in length. How many feet shy of a half mile is the racetrack? (Erroneous Petronius's answer is 200.)

   _____ feet

2. The Circus Maximus can seat 250,000 spectators. The Colosseum can accommodate only a fifth of that number. How many people can squeeze into the Colosseum?

   (Erroneous Petronius arrives at an answer of 40,000.)

   _____ people

3. A charioteer named Gaius Appuleius Diocles won 1,462 of the 4,257 races he entered in his career. In round numbers, what percentage of the races he entered did he win? (Erroneous Petronius maintains that he won 25%, but Erroneous, as usual, is wrong.)

   _____ %

4. Gaius Appuleius Diocles raced for 24 years. In round numbers, how many races did he win on average in a year? (Erroneous came up with an answer of almost 70.)

   _____ races

Classes and Occupations

ost ancient societies could be divided into two very large groups: the "haves" and the "have-nots." The "haves," of course, were the upper classes, generally consisting of rulers, nobles, and priests. The "have-nots" was made up mostly of merchants, artisans, and peasants. Although merchants and artisans were far better off than lowly peasants, they were still considered inferior to the upper classes. In every ancient civilization, there was a large slave class at the bottom of the social structure.

The burial mask of Pharaoh Tutankhamen, known in history as King Tut. Like all pharaohs, Tutankhamen had absolute power.

In ancient Egypt there were four social classes. At the top was the royal family, along with a large number of nobles and priests. Next came a class of professional soldiers, followed by a middle class consisting of merchants, artisans, and scribes (recordkeepers). At the bottom were the peasants, who were mostly farmers. Some peasants labored in cities or worked either in rock quarries or in copper and turquoise mines. At the bottom, of course, were the slaves, many of whom had been brought to Egypt as prisoners of war. Other slaves were people who sold themselves to escape debt or foreigners who had come to Egypt.

The ruler of ancient Egypt was the pharaoh, a title that meant "great house." The pharaoh had absolute power and was believed to be a god on earth. He was very pampered, being waited upon by numerous aides, generals, launderers, and other courtly figures. Records show that twenty officials, including barbers, hairdressers, manicurists, and perfumers—were required to handle his daily dressing. The perfumers thoroughly deodorized the pharaoh's body and colored his eyelids, cheeks, and lips with cosmetics. Some court attendants carried such lofty titles as "Overseer of the Cosmetic Box" and "Overseer of the Cosmetic Pencil."

The most powerful figure below the pharaoh was the vizier. The vizier was a combination prime minister, chief justice, and head of the treasury. Next came the governors of the provinces, along with various other nobles and a large class of priests. Below these worthies were the professional soldiers who maintained order throughout the empire.

Foremost among the middle class were the scribes. Scribes were officials who handled such duties as keeping records and going over tax returns.

From *Everyday Life: Ancient Times* © 2006 Good Year Books.

Because they had gone to special schools, they were usually the only Egyptians who could read and write. Their services were also in great demand as writers and readers of personal letters.

Merchants and artisans, and the peasants below them, all had occupations that were similar to castes. Sons were expected to follow in the footsteps of their fathers and pursue the same endeavors. Slaves had very different lives, depending on whether they worked in a household or in the mines or at other hard labor. Ironically, it was probably easier for slaves to better their lot than for anyone else in society. Many gained their freedom and became quite prominent.

Classes in Mesopotamia mirrored those in Egypt. Although set up a little differently, there were still upper, middle, and lower classes. At the top was the aristocracy, made up of the richest and most powerful families of the region. From the aristocracy came all the high-ranking officials, counselors, priests, soldiers, and ambassadors of the government, as well as the generals of the army. The wealth and power of the aristocracy stemmed from their huge holdings of land, which often exceeded hundreds of acres.

Lumped into the commoner, or "free," class were farmers, merchants, scribes, fishermen, herdsmen, and a variety of craftsmen. Many craftsmen worked solely for wealthy landlords. Others engaged in private enterprise, in which they were free to sell their services and wares in the open market.

At the bottom of the Mesopotamian social order were the slaves and the serfs. Serfs were peasants who farmed the land. They had to turn over their harvest to a noble, who granted them a miserable ration of food. Many Mesopotamian slaves could attribute their fate to debt. A father could sell his children or his entire family (or even himself) to pay off what he owed. Even so, slaves were not mistreated and even possessed certain rights. They could take part in business, borrow money, and even purchase their own freedom.

In Greece, social classes varied from city-state to city-state. In general, however, classes were based on citizenship. In both Athens and Sparta, children whose parents were citizens became citizens by birth and were therefore part of the upper class and had the right to participate in Greek democratic institutions. Women were also citizens, but they possessed no political rights.

Next in rank were resident aliens (many of them Greeks from other city-states), or noncitizens, most of whom were artisans and merchants. In Athens, such noncitizens were called *metics*. In Sparta, they were referred to as *perioikoi*. Though free to come and go as they pleased, neither the metics or the perioikoi

could own property or exercise full civil rights. And they could not hope to become citizens. Remember that citizenship in both Athens and Sparta was determined by birth.

At the bottom of the Greek social order were masses of slaves. The manner in which these unfortunates were treated depended on the particular city-state. In Athens, slaves were seldom abused. A master did not have the power of life and death over his slaves, nor could he subject them to brutal treatment. A master could, if he chose, free a slave, who then became a freeman, achieving a status similar to that of metics.

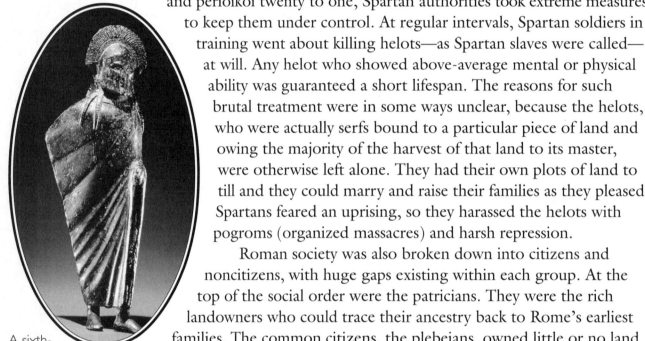

Spartan slaves were not so fortunate. Because they outnumbered citizens and perioikoi twenty to one, Spartan authorities took extreme measures to keep them under control. At regular intervals, Spartan soldiers in training went about killing helots—as Spartan slaves were called— at will. Any helot who showed above-average mental or physical ability was guaranteed a short lifespan. The reasons for such brutal treatment were in some ways unclear, because the helots, who were actually serfs bound to a particular piece of land and owing the majority of the harvest of that land to its master, were otherwise left alone. They had their own plots of land to till and they could marry and raise their families as they pleased. Spartans feared an uprising, so they harassed the helots with pogroms (organized massacres) and harsh repression.

Roman society was also broken down into citizens and noncitizens, with huge gaps existing within each group. At the top of the social order were the patricians. They were the rich landowners who could trace their ancestry back to Rome's earliest families. The common citizens, the plebeians, owned little or no land and were mostly farmers, shopkeepers, and laborers. They also had fewer political rights, being barred, for example, from serving in the senate or serving in court. About 10 percent of the population belonged to the patrician class while some 90 percent constituted the plebeians. The word *plebeian* comes from a Latin word meaning "the masses." Today, first-year students at U.S. military service academies are referred to as "plebes" after this Roman term.

A sixth-century BC bronze figurine depicting a Spartan soldier. The military were the highest social class in Sparta.

In time, the plebeians began agitating for more equality. Plebeians gained political rights, and a law was passed allowing the two groups to intermarry. There was also a small middle class of the equestrians, or "knights." They were originally the monarch's cavalrymen (only well-off men could afford to keep

From *Everyday Life: Ancient Times* © 2006 Good Year Books.

horses). Gradually, most of them migrated into business, forming a merchant class. Over time, the patricians, equestrians, and a few wealthy plebeians merged into an aristocractic class, and the distinctions between them disappeared. A political party, the Populares ("on the people's side"), emerged to represent the common people, and in response the aristocracy formed the Optimates ("the best class") to try and maintain their privilege.

After the Roman Republic fell, things again became worse for the common people. They lost the rights they had gained and became known as the *humiliores,* in contrast to the *honestiores,* basically the privileged classes. Under the Republic, all men were supposedly equal under the law, but under the Empire, the humiliores received harsher sentences than honestiores for the same crimes.

In early India, the caste system that came to be associated with that country did not develop for many centuries. At first, Indian society was divided into three classes consisting of the rich and powerful, a middle class of merchants and farmers, and a lower class of workers and slaves. Then, sometime around 1500 BC, a group of people called the *Aryans* moved into the Indus Valley and established the caste system along with the origins of the Hindu religion. There were some 3,000 castes, divided into four classes. The first class consisted of the Brahmans, or priests, followed in order by the nobles and warriors (Kshatriyas), the merchants, farmers, and traders (Vaishyas), and the Sudras. The latter group included all artisans and unskilled workers. At the very bottom of Indian society was a group not belonging to any caste. They were known as the *untouchables* and performed jobs considered polluting, such as that of butchers or street sweepers.

China had nothing resembling a caste system. At the top, below the ruler, was a class of great feudal lords who governed the land in his name. Next came a class of knightly gentry, or landowners, who served at court and fought in the armies of the feudal lords. At the bottom were the peasants on whose labor everyone relied. Merchants and artisans, like slaves, were not recognized as belonging to any class. For the most part, it appears that these groups were simply tolerated.

A fresco from the first-century AD depicting a Roman slave combing a girl's hair. Slaves made up more than one-third of ancient Rome's population.

Name _____ Date _____

Name Those Ancient Persons

In the word box are names associated with members of certain occupations, positions, and classes of ancient times. Select the correct term from the box and write it on the blank line in front of each statement.

Brahman
equestrian
helot
humiliore
metic
optimate
Overseer of the Cosmetic Box
patrician
perioikoi
pharaoh
plebeian
scribe
Sudra
untouchable
vizier

1. _____ This was my title as ruler of Egypt.

2. _____ I was an unskilled worker in India.

3. _____ I was a member of the upper class in early Rome.

4. _____ I was a noncitizen of Athens.

5. _____ This was my title as prime minister of Egypt.

6. _____ I belong to no Indian caste.

7. _____ I was a member of the early Roman lower classes.

8. _____ I kept records and wrote letters in ancient Egypt.

9. _____ This name was given to priests in India.

10. _____ I was a member of this political party, formed to protect the privileges of the Roman aristocracy.

11. _____ This name was given to commoners such as I in the latter days of Rome.

12. _____ I was a Spartan serf.

13. _____ I assisted the pharaoh in his daily dress.

14. _____ We were the noncitizens of Sparta.

15. _____ This name was given to myself and others of the Roman merchant class.

From *Everyday Life: Ancient Times* © 2006 Good Year Books.

Name _____ Date _____

Distinguish between Fact and Opinion

Can you tell a fact from an opinion? A fact is something known to be true. An opinion is simply what someone thinks.

Carefully read the sentences on this page. Then in the blank line to the left of each, write F if you think the statement is a fact or O if you consider it an opinion.

1. _____ No people in modern times have had it worse than the slaves of ancient societies.

2. _____ Few rulers today enjoy the power held by the kings and emperors of past civilizations.

3. _____ Few people in ancient times could read or write.

4. _____ The helots of Sparta probably suffered more than any group of people in history.

5. _____ Citizenship in Athens and Sparta was based solely on birth.

6. _____ Women everywhere today have more rights than the women of ancient times.

7. _____ Because they were so outnumbered and in constant danger, Spartans were justified in their periodic slaying of helots.

8. _____ Merchants and artisans in ancient China were not recognized as belonging to any social class.

9. _____ Invaders called *Aryans* established the caste system in India.

10. _____ Only about 10 percent of early Romans belonged to the patrician class.

11. _____ Slaves in ancient societies accepted their lowly status without question or resistance.

12. _____ Excessive pampering made most Egyptian pharaohs lazy and incompetent.

13. _____ Metics in Athens had no hope of becoming citizens.

14. _____ Unemployed persons in the latter days of the Roman Empire were content to live off government handouts.

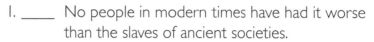

Name _____ Date _____

Make an Outline

Make an outline depicting the social classes of early Egypt, Mesopotamia, India, and China.

I. Egypt

II. Mesopotamia

III. India

IV. China

From *Everyday Life: Ancient Times* © 2006 Good Year Books.

Name _____ Date _____

Play the Devil's Advocate

Have you ever played the "devil's advocate"? If so, you might have supported an unpopular cause simply for the sake of argument.

At some point in your school career, you will probably be asked to participate in a debate and to defend a point or issue with which you completely disagree. This activity provides you with a little "on-the-job" training for such a likely event.

On the lines provided, create a dialogue with another person in which you point out reasons why ancient societies were justified in making slaves of conquered peoples. Remember: No matter how strongly you feel about the institution of slavery, you must come up with reasons why past civilizations were right in upholding it.

_____
_____
_____
_____
_____
_____
_____
_____
_____
_____
_____
_____
_____
_____
_____
_____
_____
_____

Transportation and Communication

hroughout history, transportation and communication have been closely linked to water travel. Towns and settlements sprang up along rivers and other waterways that afforded cheap and easy means of transport. It is no surprise, therefore, that history's earliest civilizations—those of Egypt, Mesopotamia, India, and China—developed and grew in close proximity to mighty rivers. Even the city-states of Greece and the city of Rome were built in areas where water travel was accessible.

Carved tablet showing a trireme. Triremes were the standard warships of ancient times.

Egyptians were fortunate that the Nile River flows through the length of their country. They were also fortunate that, while the Nile flows from south to north, prevailing winds blow in the opposite direction. Thus, a boatman could drift down river with the current and then use his sail to travel back. The first images of ships with sales come from Egypt. Crafts ranging in size from small papyrus skiffs (small, light boats) to ships 200 feet long traveled down and up the river to all parts of Egypt.

Land transportation was at first a matter of walking. People simply struck out on foot. If they had goods to transport, they carried them on their backs. Later travelers and goods began to be moved by donkey. About 1674 BC, invaders called the *Hyksos* introduced the horse and chariot to Egypt, after which those with the means to do so went about in wheeled transport.

In addition to innovations in transportation, ancient Egyptians were the first to make use of a regular postal system. Couriers or messengers delivered letters anywhere in the kingdom within a matter of weeks. Messages and letters were written on papyrus, a writing material made from the pith of a river reed. (Parts of this same reed were used to make the papyrus skiffs that traveled the Nile River.) Egyptians who could not write could either hire a scribe or dictate a message to a carrier, who would deliver the letter verbally.

The Mesopotamians, like the Egyptians, built long, narrow galleys for plying the open seas. Typical galleys were about 60 feet long and were

From *Everyday Life: Ancient Times* © 2006 GoodYear Books.

propelled by both a sail and oars. For traveling up and down rivers, the usual Mesopotamian craft was a small rowboat that resembled a tub. It was built of reed covered with animal skin and was pushed along by large oars. This strange-looking boat was used to carry grain and textiles between cities.

With regard to land transportation, the Mesopotamians were the first people to use wheeled vehicles. Sometime around 3500 BC, the Sumerians invented the wheel, which led to the appearance of chariots, carts, and wagons. Until the appearance of the horse, chariots were drawn by onagers, wild beasts that resembled donkeys. For many years, only nobles and priests used wheeled vehicles. Later, wheels were attached to carts and wagons for use by the common people.

Roads in Mesopotamia were short and few in number until the advent of the Persian Empire. The last people to occupy Mesopotamia before the rise of the Greeks and Romans, the Persians constructed the first extensive road system in the sixth century BC. One road, known as the Royal Highway, ran 1,500 miles from the Persian Gulf to the Aegean Sea. The Persians also continued the postal system that had been started several centuries earlier by the Assyrians.

Roads were even worse in mountainous Greece, making overland travel difficult. Most roads were narrow, designed for pedestrians or pack animals. Most roads were simply scraped down to the underlying rock, although sections might be paved with stones where necessary. Particularly on steep hills or patches of uneven ground, cartwheel ruts were sometimes cut into the surface to give carts more stability and better traction.

Water travel was easier. A common Greek merchant ship was the holkas. It was powered almost exclusively by sails, meaning they could be virtually stalled by unfavorable winds. Broad, deep ships, holkades (the plural of holkas) were not designed for speed, but could haul substantial amounts of cargo. Loads of 150 tons were common, and some ships carried twice that.

The Greeks also had ships designed specifically for war. An early type was the bireme, which appeared around 700 BC. This galley had a single square sail but its primary power came from two banks of rowers along each side of the ship. A few centuries later, the trireme appeared.

The trireme had three rows of oars and carried a crew of 170 rowers. The trireme was about 115 feet long and was steered by a pair of paddles at the stern. It was relatively light, being capable of attaining speeds from 7 to 10 knots over short distances.

These fast ships were used almost exclusively for war. Each trireme was equipped at the bow with a metal-topped battering ram for sinking enemy ships. Sketches show these rams as being colorful and decorative—decorative, that is, to all except an adversary. Once an enemy vessel was rammed, it quickly sank and most of its crew drowned.

Unlike earlier peoples, the Greeks did not have a postal system. Instead, news was either flashed by fire beacons from hill to hill or sent by carrier pigeon. Couriers carried messages from place to place and delivered them by word of mouth. Sometimes, important messages were also conveyed by runners. You may have studied about Pheidippides, a famous runner of Athens. He is remembered for having run nonstop from the plain of Marathon to Athens—a distance of about 26 miles—to inform the inhabitants of a great victory over the Persians. Upon reaching the gates of the city and shouting, "Rejoice, victory is ours," he is said to have died on the spot. The name for our modern marathon race is derived from Pheidippides' feat.

No ancient people found travel easier than the Romans. This was because the Roman government built an excellent system of roads throughout the empire. On these roads, the upper classes traveled in style in carriages with drivers, while commoners went about either on foot or on horses and mules. Some 53,000 miles of roads connected the various provinces to Rome. The best of these were so well constructed that some are still in use today.

An engraving showing a portion of the Appian Way.

The oldest and most prominent road was the Appian Way. Begun in 312 BC, it at first ran from Rome to Capua. Later it was extended to Brundisium on Italy's southeast coast. All told, it stretched for 360 miles. The Appian Way was about as wide as a two-lane highway and was constructed of lava laid on a bed of mortared stone. Parts of the road are still traveled today.

Like other ancient peoples, the Romans had a postal system. But their outstanding achievement in communication might have been the *Acta Diurna* (Daily Events), an innovation hailed by some historians as the world's first newspaper. Attributed to Julius Caesar and started in Rome in 59 BC, the *Acta Diurna* listed important new laws and events, as well as births and deaths. Other cities also began to post announcements.

About the same time as the Romans were building their imperial road system, so were the Chinese, completing a network that covered about 25,000 miles by the end of ancient times. Paved with stone and tree-lined, these roads linked the empire. Some of the bridges on them were so well constructed that they survive today. The Chinese also dug a network of canals connecting the major rivers. The greatest of these canals was the Grand Canal, which ran 1,085 miles between the cities of Hang-chow and Beijing—a distance equivalent to that from New York to Florida. As an engineering wonder, it is surpassed only by the Great Wall of China.

On land, Chinese with means went about in fancy sedan chairs carried on the shoulders of hired servants or rode in horse-drawn carriages. Common people usually walked, and when they had to transport a load, they often utilized large bundles or heavy buckets balanced on the ends of poles and slung over the shoulder. Sometimes they carried goods in carts pulled by oxen or donkeys.

Transportation in India was also highly advanced. People, chariots, carts, sedan chairs, horses, camels, and elephants traveled on an imperial system of well-constructed highways. One imperial highway that was 1,200 miles in length had, at regular intervals, shade trees, water wells, and the ancient equivalents of hotels and police stations. These highways, along with more narrow trade routes and even narrower village roads, were built and maintained by a ministry of public works.

Few ancient societies could match the transportation system established in India. Some of the roads built by the Indian government rivaled those of Rome.

From Everyday Life: Ancient Times © 2006 Good Year Books.

Name _____ Date _____

Create a Bar Graph of Your Own

Use the data about ancient travel routes presented on the page and create a bar graph of your own. At the bottom of your graph, make up several word problems associated with it. Ask a classmate to solve the problems.

Road	Location	Length in Miles
Appian Way	Rome	360
Royal Highway	Persia	1,500
An Imperial Highway	India	1,200
Flaminium Way	Rome	120
Grand Canal	China	1,085

_____
_____
_____
_____
_____
_____

From Everyday Life: Ancient Times © 2006 Good Year Books.

Name _____ Date _____

Solve a Transportation Puzzle

Fill in the sentences for clues to complete the puzzle about transportation in ancient times.

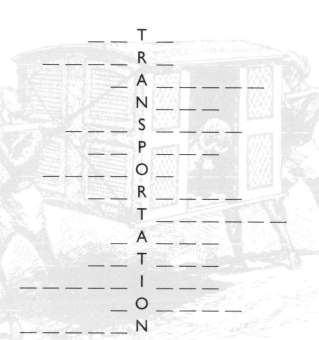

```
_ _ T _
_ _ _ _ _ R _ _
      A
_ _ _ _ S _ _ _ _
      P
_ _ _ _ _ O _
      R
_ _ _ _ _ T _ _ _ _
      A
_ _ _ _ I _ _
      O
_ _ _ _ _ N
```

1. The _____ Diurna was an early Roman newspaper.

2. The wealthy in some ancient societies rode about in sedan _____.

3. _____ was a river reed from which paper was made.

4. The _____ River flows from south to north through Egypt.

5. The _____ traveled over a well-built road called the *Royal Highway*.

6. The first Roman road of note was the _____ Way.

7. The _____ introduced the chariot to Egypt.

8. _____ often wrote letters for people in ancient Egypt.

9. The _____ was a warship having three rows of oars.

10. The Grand _____ is an engineering marvel of ancient China.

11. Pheidippedes ran from the plain of _____ to Athens.

12. The _____ invented the wheel.

13. The Greek merchant ship was called a _____.

14. The Royal Highway extended from the Persian Gulf to the _____ sea.

Name _____ Date _____

Keep a Traveler's Diary

Imagine yourself living in Roman times and making a two-day trip by mule along the Appian Way. Make up diary entries for the two days. Think of occurrences that could have taken place on such a journey.

Junius 5

Dear Diary,

_____

_____

_____

_____

_____

_____

_____

_____

_____

_____

Junius 6

Dear Diary,

_____

_____

_____

_____

_____

_____

_____

_____

_____

_____

From *Everyday Life: Ancient Times* © 2006 Good Year Books.

Name _____ Date _____

Compare and Contrast Two Eras

You have learned that travel and communication in ancient times were primitive compared to modern means of transportation.

On the chart below, compare means of travel, postal service, and communication in ancient times with today's methods.

Ancient Times

Travel _____

_____

_____

_____

_____

_____

Postal Service _____

_____

_____

_____

_____

_____

Other Means of Communication _____

_____

_____

_____

_____

Today

Travel _____

_____

_____

_____

_____

_____

Postal Service _____

_____

_____

_____

_____

_____

Other Means of Communication _____

_____

_____

_____

_____

Education and Religion

In ancient times education was—for children of the common people—largely vocational in nature. Boys learned the trades of their fathers, and mothers taught girls household responsibilities. Sometimes girls also helped in the fields, planting and harvesting crops.

The schools that existed in ancient societies were only for the children of the upper classes. Except in Greece and Rome, these schools were almost always attached to temples, where the instructors were priests. Discipline was harsh and expectations were high. For the most part, only boys attended. Some societies allowed girls to be educated, although rarely to the same extent as boys.

Cuneiform writing, which was made up of many wedge-shaped characters.

In ancient Egypt, girls did not attend school, although they could apprentice in certain professions. Boys destined to become scribes or public officials (usually because their fathers were) received an education, beginning at age four or five. All students learned reading and writing and played sports. Some learned such subjects as geography, mathematics, or foreign languages as needed for their future professions. An important purpose of education was to teach good manners and morals, including respect for one's elders. As such, instructor-priests felt that young boys listened better when beaten. "A student's ear is on his back," the priests like to point out. "He hears when he is beaten." Apparently such methods reaped results; one pupil wrote to his former teacher, "Thou didst beat my back, and thy instructions went into my ear."

Most boys who attended Egyptian temple schools studied to become scribes. This was no easy task, considering that hieroglyphics, the Egyptian form of picture-writing, contained more than two thousand characters to be memorized. Plus, scribes had to learn a type of cursive, called *hieratic,* for everyday business and letter writing. (And you probably thought that having to cope with twenty-six letters in the first grade was torture!) The future scribe studied from sunrise to sunset and had little time for leisure activities. If he did well, he was guaranteed a good job and a good life.

From *Everyday Life: Ancient Times* © 2006 Good Year Books.

Schools in Mesopotamia were similar to those in Egypt. Only boys attended, and they usually studied to become scribes. Discipline may have been more severe than in Egypt. The preferred method of administering punishment was the cane, and teachers and monitors looked for any excuse to let a student have it. One boy complained to his father that he had been caned nine times in one day! His misdeeds ranged from failing to do his assignments to loitering in the street.

Students in Mesopotamian schools had to learn a form of picture-writing called *cuneiform.* It consisted of several hundred wedge-shaped characters pressed into wet, clay tablets with a writing tool called a *stylus.* Cuneiform was as difficult to read as it was to write. Some characters stood for syllables; others represented whole words. And everything looked like points or triangles.

Although cuneiform was also inscribed on stone or papyrus, our main source of information about this ancient language comes from the more than twenty thousand clay tablets found at Nineveh on the Tigris River. Here the Assyrian king Ashurbanipal built a huge library containing the writings of the Sumerians and Babylonians, as well as those of his own people. Today this library of priceless tablets is stored in the British Museum in London.

This tomb painting includes an image of Egyptian girls playing the harp and lute.

Throughout Greece, education was designed with one purpose in mind: to teach young people (mostly boys) to become good citizens. What was included in the curriculum depended on each city-state's definition of good citizenship. In Sparta, a good citizen spent his entire life in the army and accepted without question strict discipline and a regimented life. Thus, the curriculum of a Spartan school centered around physical training. Both boys and girls lived at barracks-like schools from the age of seven and went through a vigorous program of physical fitness.

In Athens and other city-states, most male citizens could read by about 400 BC; schools offered such subjects as logic (reasoning), writing, arithmetic, and physical education with music, poetry, and art thrown in for good measure. Girls could receive an education, although they probably were mostly taught at home by the mothers. Girls' schooling focused on "domestic science," or how to run a good household.

From Everyday Life: Ancient Times © 2006 Good Year Books.

Parents had to pay for their children to go to school, but fees were low because teachers—who were usually slaves or freedmen—received little pay. These underpaid teachers were sent boys from the ages of six to fourteen. Each boy was accompanied by his paidagogos, a slave who looked after him. If the boy was late to class, he could expect a good flogging from his teacher. His paidagogos was often flogged too, for not getting his young charge to school on time. Do you think Greek students were late very often? Some students pursued higher education from private tutors. Later on, several teachers—like Plato and Aristotle—set up their own centers of learning, often in public gymnasiums.

Education in Rome was also private; because parents had to pay, most poor children had little or no education. Roman students, like their Greek counterparts, attended classes in any available space. Some teachers held classes in the streets, while others set up shop in their homes or rented rooms.

From the ages of seven to eleven, both boys and girls in Rome went to school. Girls were accompanied by a nurse and boys by a pedagogue, a slave like Greek boys had. They studied reading, writing, and arithmetic. All learning was by rote, which meant that students went over lessons again and again until they were memorized. Discipline was strict, and inattentive or disruptive students could expect a cuff on the ear.

Formal education ended for most girls at age eleven, when they began preparing for marriage. But boys moved on to something similar to modern high schools. There they studied history, geography, astronomy, music, Greek, and Latin. The purpose of secondary school was to prepare young men to learn rhetoric, or the art of public speaking. This was a must for the more prestigious professions.

In ancient India, elementary education took place at home. Between the ages of eight and twelve, depending on his caste, a boy left home to live with a guru, or teacher. This person treated the boy like his own son and gave him a free education in exchange for the boy doing the household chores. Boys learned such subjects as religion, grammar, philosophy, and arithmetic, although each boy's education was tailored to the needs of his caste. The boy was expected to live up to the high moral standards of his religion (Hinduism) by living almost like a monk.

When he was sixteen, and if he was qualified, he might move on to one of India's universities. It is interesting that ancient India, at a time when European civilization had not even begun, had institutions of higher learning.

From *Everyday Life: Ancient Times* © 2006 Good Year Books.

In time, this system, which favored the Brahman caste, broke down. Schoolmasters opened schools in nearly every Indian village. The same education was available to every caste except the Sudras. If you remember, the Sudras were the serfs of Indian society. Not only were they denied an education, but they were forbidden to learn the Vedas, the sacred writings of the Hindus, or to participate in some religious ceremonies.

In early China, the various feudal lords established schools in their capital cities for the sons of nobles. These schools taught a curriculum of rituals, archery, charioteering, writing, and mathematics. An important part of education was teaching good character and morals, especially honoring one's father and ancestors. There were separate elementary schools in the various villages for boys of common folk, and there were schools the adults could attend at night after their work in the fields. Girls received a separate education focused on domestic skills. Students who wished to continue beyond an elementary education attached themselves to some learned sage (wise person) who was willing to teach them.

Until Christianity became the official religion of the Roman Empire in the year 380, the religions of all ancient peoples were polytheistic in nature. *Polytheism* refers to the belief in and worship of many gods. There were national gods, local gods, and household gods. Some ancient societies, such as that of the Chinese, also engaged in ancestor worship.

Space does not permit a detailed study of the many religions, gods, and goddesses, of ancient civilizations. But we will mention a few with whom you are probably familiar. In Greece, there was Zeus, the chief god; Aphrodite, the goddess of love and beauty; Poseidon, the god of the sea; and Athena, the goddess of wisdom. The Romans adopted many Greek gods and simply changed their names. Zeus became Jupiter; Aphrodite, Venus; Poseidon, Neptune; and Athena, Minerva. Some important gods and goddesses of ancient Egypt were Re (or Ra), the sun god; Osiris, the god of the Underworld and Isis, his wife, a goddess of nature; and Nut (no kidding!), the goddess of the sky and Osiris's mother. Marduk was a chief god among the Babylonians, one of the many peoples who established kingdoms and empires in Mesopotamia. Ancient civilizations invented a long array of gods and goddesses as a way of explaining natural phenomena and events they did not understand.

The Greeks called this goddess Athena, while the Romans called her Minerva.

Name _____ Date _____

Use Your Critical Thinking Skills

Think about these questions. Then write your best answer to each on the lines provided.

1. Until recent times, schools relied on corporal punishment (such as spanking) to discipline unruly students. Today, corporal punishment, for the most part, is no longer permitted.

   a. How do you personally feel about corporal punishment? Was it ever justified? Do you think it was effective?

   _____
   _____
   _____
   _____

   b. Do you think corporal punishment will ever be used again as a major means of discipline? Why or why not?

   _____
   _____
   _____
   _____

2. Students in ancient schools learned mainly by rote. In other words, they memorized information with little thought to its meaning.

   a. Is learning by rote an effective means of instruction? Explain your answer.

   _____
   _____
   _____
   _____

   b. Are some lessons today best learned by rote? Explain.

   _____
   _____
   _____
   _____

From *Everyday Life: Ancient Times* © 2006 Good Year Books.

Name _____ Date _____

Compare Ancient and Modern Schools

On the lines below the headings "Ancient Schools" and "Modern Schools," write pertinent facts about each.

	Ancient Schools	**Modern Schools**
1. School buildings		
2. Subjects taught		
3. Purpose of education		
4. Who attended		
5. Teachers		
6. Discipline		
7. Education for girls		
8. Students' ages		
9. Teaching methods		

Name _____ Date _____

Participate in a Skit

(A Teacher-directed Activity)

Divide the class into three groups. Each group should choose one of the skits listed. Students should use their imagination and creative skills in planning their skit. Each skit should be about five minutes in length.

Any student in a group not participating directly in a skit can either help make simple props or critique skits and rate them at the conclusion of the activity. There is a lead-in to each skit to help students in their planning.

These are just a few suggestions for skits. You can probably think of others yourself.

Skit 1: A Young Lad Complaining to His Parents and Siblings about the Difficulty of Learning Hieroglyphics

Seth is a young Egyptian boy who goes to a village school run by a local scribe. (Not every school was attached to a temple.) He is struggling to learn the two thousand characters that make up hieroglyphics. He is not happy and wishes his life were different. Create a skit centered around his discussing the problem with his family.

Skit 2: A Greek Paidegogos Upbraiding His Young Charge for Being Late to School

Poor Anaximedes! Because Leander, his young master, was slow getting ready this morning, he was thirty minutes late to class. As a result, both Leander and Anaximedes received a good flogging from Leander's teacher.

Create a skit in which Anaximedes scolds his master for being so slow. Have three or four other students standing around, making derisive comments and laughing at Leander.

Skit 3: Several Roman Girls Lamenting the Fact That Their Formal Education Has Ended

Three twelve-year-old Roman girls have just completed their studies at the equivalent of our modern elementary school. Now while their male friends move on to schools of higher learning, the girls must stay home and prepare to get married.

Center this skit around a dialogue the girls have in which they consider such an educational practice discriminatory.

From Everyday Life: Ancient Times © 2006 Good Year Books.

Name _____ Date _____

Unscramble and Identify Nouns

Listed are a group of nouns from chapter 8 whose spelling is scrambled. Unscramble each and write the correct spelling on the line next to it. On the following line, either identify, define, or explain the word.

1. SPHERIOGLICHY _____

   _____

2. URUG _____

   _____

3. FUNORMICE _____

   _____

4. SUSLYT _____

   _____

5. BRAINSHUPALA _____

   _____

6. OGADGOEPSI _____

   _____

7. DRAUS _____

   _____

8. MISTHEYPOL _____

   _____

9. OOPSDINE _____

   _____

10. MISHDUIN _____

    _____

11. THIDAROPE _____

    _____

Law and Justice

Historians differ as to how laws first developed. One group believes that laws grew out of a need for protection of life and property. They maintain that when people first appeared on earth they did as they pleased, provided they could get away with it. For example, if Zog, who lived one cave down from Thag, coveted Thag's state-of-the-art club, he might simply go to Thag's cave, punch him in the nose, and make off with the object of his desire. And if Thag was smaller than Zog, there was little he could do about it.

Hammurabi receiving his great law code from the Babylonian god Shamash.

Not so, say other scholars. They believe that from the start, people worked out rules for living together peacefully. They hold that early peoples realized that laws were needed not only for order and security but for purposes such as settling disputes, establishing governments, and providing for the poor and needy, to name a few. You can no doubt think of other reasons why laws are necessary in society.

Some of the earliest laws known to humankind were written in Egypt about 2500 BC. These laws were fair and applied equally to all classes, but the punishments for breaking them were unusually harsh. Lucky offenders might only be beaten with a rod or have their nose, ears, hands, or tongue cut off. Those less fortunate might be strangled, beheaded, eaten by crocodiles, or burned. Not only suspects but witnesses could be beaten to obtain a confession.

The first written law code to have survived the ravages of time is the famous Code of Hammurabi. Hammurabi was a Babylonian king who ruled almost four thousand years ago. Sometime around 1750 BC, he collected all of his legal decisions and had them engraved on a large stone 8 feet high. All told, there were 3,614 lines of cuneiform writing that covered 282 legal subjects. Some laws dealt with property rights and business. Others addressed criminal acts, while still others were concerned with marriage and divorce and the welfare of widows, orphans, and the poor.

Before you get the idea that Hammurabi was a decent sort who was far ahead of his time regarding law and justice, a quick look at a few pertinent facts will change your mind. Punishment for violating any of Hammurabi's laws was based on the rather primitive concept of "an eye for an eye, a tooth for a tooth." Anyone who suffered at the hands of another was entitled to retribution. Common punishments included fines, mutilation, and death. There was no such thing as imprisonment.

Regardless of Hammurabi's claim that the code provided justice for everyone, punishment varied from class to class. If a noble "broke another noble's bone or plucked out his eye," then he could expect to sacrifice a bone or eye himself. If, however, the injured party happened to be a commoner, then the guilty noble only had to pay a fine. And if the injured party was a lowly slave, the fine was so low it was almost laughable. This unequal concept also applied to theft; anyone guilty of stealing who did not have the means to reimburse the victim was put to death. If, however, the thief was a person of means, all he had to do was repay the amount stolen — with a little extra thrown in — and his punishment was considered over.

Punishments for breaking other laws in Hammurabi's Code were just as severe. If, for example, a contractor built a house that collapsed and killed any of its occupants, he was put to death. If a son struck his father, his fingers were cut off. Hands and other body parts were also sacrificed by doctors who performed unsuccessful operations or nurses who somehow managed to switch babies at birth. And so it went.

Harsh as it was, the Code of Hammurabi represented a step forward in that it standardized laws and punishments throughout the land. In spite of its inequities, it took the position that a person was innocent until proven guilty. It also provided stiff penalties for dishonest judges and for anyone who tried to bribe a judge. The code continued to be the basis for law in the Near East for many years after Hammurabi died.

About five hundred years later, what is often called the Law of Moses, or Mosaic Law, came into existence. It was based on the Ten Commandments, and its influence can be seen in the laws of many nations. Although the Law of Moses also demanded "an eye for an eye" as punishment, it placed a much higher value on human life and stressed the importance of a code of moral conduct.

In the seventh century BC, the ancient Greeks also began to collect existing laws and put them in written form. One of the first was the code drawn up by the Athenian ruler Draco in 621 BC. Like those in other countries,

it was harsh, but it was different in a way characteristic of most Greek city-states: It was based on popular consent and could be changed only by a vote of the people.

These ruins are all that is left of the platform used by the Athenian Assembly. Athens was known as the "birthplace of democracy."

And that is what happened some twenty-seven years later. An elected archon, or chief officer, of Athens named Solon provided that drastic changes be made in that city-state's laws. Enslavement for debt was abolished and poor people were given a voice in their government. As a result of the latter, all citizens became members of the assembly that made the laws and elected the archons. Because Solon's laws were so wise and far-reaching, lawmakers today are often referred to as *solons*. In the fifth century BC, the Greeks also introduced jury trials as well as the right of appeal.

No ancient people made greater contributions in law than the Romans. Although Hammurabi's Code had introduced the concept that a person was innocent until proven guilty, the Romans put this principle into wide use. Two other important principles of Roman law stated that people were equal in the eyes of the law and that confessions gained by torture were not valid in a court of law. All three of these ideas were later incorporated into the legal systems of various European nations.

Roman laws were first brought together in 450 BC and inscribed on twelve bronze tablets. The contents of these tablets were called the *Law of the Twelve Tables* and were displayed in the Roman Forum (public square) for all to see and read. Basically, they dealt mostly with the rights of individuals. Some laws showed wisdom, but others, such as a Roman being forbidden to damage his neighbor's crops by the use of evil charms, appear silly to us today.

Early Roman law placed much power in the hands of the father. You have already learned that the father held the power of life and death over his children. The same held true for his wife. If a wife was guilty of being unfaithful, or if she had stolen the keys to her husband's wine cellar, he could condemn her to death or sell her into slavery.

From *Everyday Life: Ancient Times* © 2006 Good Year Books.

In time, history's first legal profession developed in Rome, and law books began to appear. The crowning achievement of Roman law was the code drawn up between AD 529 and 565 by Emperor Justinian of the eastern part of the empire. (The western part had collapsed a little earlier.) The Justinian Code was a compilation of the early Twelve Tables and the many laws and court decisions that occurred afterward. Its concepts of justice and the rights of individuals became the basis of law in a number of modern countries.

In ancient India, laws were derived from the Hindu religious texts. Cases were heard by a panchayat, or committee of five. All members of the caste group could attend. Punishment for crimes may have been even harsher than in Egypt and Mesopotamia. Mutilation, torture, and death were the usual sentences for most wrongdoings. Those convicted who were spared the death penalty still suffered the loss of some vital body part. Those put to death were executed in hideous ways.

The Chinese believed that laws came out of the natural order of the universe. As the "Son of Heaven," the emperor declared when laws had been broken and what the punishment would be. The various princes and offices under the emperor handed out punishments in his name. The possible punishments, from most to least severe, were death, cutting off the feet or kneecaps, branding, and beating. The Chinese were not concerned with personal or property rights—it was up to each head of household to govern his own family. Instead, the laws only addressed issues that affected the public's safety or well-being. In 536 BC, eighty years before the Twelve Tables of Rome were created, a Chinese statesman named Tsz-ch'an recorded the criminal laws on metal, the so-called Code in Brass. Although the code itself has been lost, its principles are still reflected in Chinese law today.

A mosaic depicting the Emperor Justinian. Justinian is remembered for compiling the laws of Rome into a code.

Name _____ Date _____

Write Your Opinions

Punishments for breaking laws in ancient times were severe. Most offenses were punishable by death. With this is mind, write your opinions to the questions opposite.

1. Do you think capital punishment (the death penalty) is justified? Why or why not?

   _____

   _____

   _____

2. Is capital punishment a deterrent to crime? Why or why not?

   _____

   _____

   _____

3. What would you suggest as an alternative to capital punishment?

   _____

   _____

   _____

4. What is your opinion of parole, or early release from prison? Is it justified? Why or why not?

   _____

   _____

   _____

5. Should youthful offenders be punished in the same way as their adult counterparts? Why or why not?

   _____

   _____

   _____

Name _____   Date _____

Write a Letter to the Editor

You learned in chapter 9 that the Ten Commandments form the cornerstone of the Law of Moses. Today, much controversy surrounds the display of the Ten Commandments in such places as schools and public buildings. Some people maintain that displaying the Commandments violates the principle of the separation of church and state and, therefore, should not be allowed. Others think that the Ten Commandments form the basis of our beliefs about behavior and morality and should be on display for all to see.

What do you think? On the lines provided, write a letter to the editor of an imaginary newspaper giving reasons why the Commandments shoulor should not be on display in public buildings.

Name _____ Date _____

Make False Statements True

All of these statements are false. Change the words in italics to make them true. Write the replacement words on the lines following the statements.

1. Laws in ancient Egypt were extremely *lenient.*
   _____

2. Hammurabi's law code was written in *hieroglyphics.*
   _____

3. The Law of Moses was based on the *Code of Hammurabi.* _____

4. *Judges* today are often referred to as "solons."
   _____

5. The Twelve Tables were inscribed on *gold* tablets.
   _____

6. The Twelve Tables were prominently displayed in the Roman *Senate.* _____

7. Punishment under Hammurabi's code was *the same for all classes.* _____

8. *Chinese* law became the basis for the legal systems of many European nations. _____

9. Chinese law today is based on the principles in the Code in *Wax.* _____

10. Justinian was an emperor of the *Babylonian* Empire.
    _____

11. Laws in ancient China came about as a result of decisions by *lawyers.* _____

12. The Greeks introduced the trial by *fire.*
    _____

13. Laws in ancient India were *no more* severe than those in China. _____

Name _____ Date _____

Complete a Before and After Page

What did you know about ancient laws before reading this chapter? Were your preconceived ideas factual or based on common misconceptions? How did your ideas change after being exposed to more information?

This page is divided into three parts. One part is labeled "What I Thought I Knew," another "What I Learned," and a third asks the question: "Were Ancient Laws Appropriate for the Times?" On the lines provided, write information about each topic.

What I Thought I Knew

_____

_____

_____

_____

_____

_____

_____

What I Learned

_____

_____

_____

_____

_____

_____

Were Ancient Laws Appropriate for the Times? Explain.

_____

_____

_____

_____

_____

_____

CHAPTER 10

Health and Medicine

Depart, cold, son of cold, thou who breakest the bones, destroyest the skull, makest ill the seven openings of the head! . . . Go out on the floor, stink, stink, stink!

If you had lived in ancient Egypt, the above incantation was guaranteed to rid the body of a cold. We know, of course, that such magical words had no effect on one of humankind's most nagging illnesses. In all fairness to the Egyptians, however, it was probably not much less effective than the dozens of over-the-counter cold remedies that we stock our shelves with today.

Most historians agree that medical science began in ancient Egypt. The sick were treated by doctors—priests with specialized medical and religious knowledge. They set broken bones with splints and casts and closed open wounds with sutures and clamps. But they also provided magic potions and rituals. Both were considered equally effective, and the choice between them depended on whether the cause of the ailment was visible (like a broken bone) or not (like a virus). Thus, medicine in ancient Egypt was a strange mixture of knowledge and superstition.

Doctors in ancient Egypt correctly recognized the importance of the heart to the workings of the body. They were also the first to perform surgery on a variety of ailments. Records have been found that explain in detail forty-eight cases of surgery, each carefully detailed from diagnosis to treatment. Many doctors specialized in one field. Some focused on obstetrics or gynecology, while others treated disorders of the stomach and the like. In addition, there were many general practitioners who treated patients for everything from baldness to sore toes.

On the downside, Egyptian medicine was strongly influenced by magic and superstition. Doctors relied on potions so vile and repugnant that they defy description. Salves, poultices, and prescriptions were designed to make a patient's body unattractive to demons. A typical potion might include some or

An Egyptian physician pouring medicine that was believed to treat blindness.

From *Everyday Life: Ancient Times* © 2006 Good Year Books.

all of the following: garlic, honey, lead, soot, cow bile, lizard's blood, swine's ears and teeth, tortoise brains, and an old book boiled in oil!

Medicine as practiced in Mesopotamia was also a mixture of scientific knowledge and magic; there were separate doctors (asu) and sorcerers (ashipu). Illness was thought to be caused by spirits or some evil the patient had done. The ashipu's job was to determine which demon caused the illness and whether rational or magical treatment would be most effective. Although doctors could consult manuals and textbooks containing diagnoses and treatment for many illnesses, they were reluctant to perform surgery for fear of uncomfortable repercussions. Hammurabi's Code specifically stated that if a doctor operated on a patient of high status and the surgery was successful, he was to be paid ten shekels. For operating on a slave, he received only two. But if the operation failed to correct the high-status patient's problem, the surgeon was expected to sacrifice a hand! (He merely had to replace the slave.) Under the circumstances, it is easy to see why the operating table remained largely unoccupied. Physicians did know about many herbal remedies that had antibiotic or antiseptic properties.

In Mesopotamia sorcerers were in greater demand than physicians. Some of the concoctions that these pseudo-doctors mixed up to drive out evil spirits included, among other things, rotten food, raw meat, fat, dirt, crushed bones, snake flesh, and wood shavings. If these vile-smelling remedies did not bring about the desired results, sorcerers sometimes appealed to the better side of demons (they actually believed demons had better sides) and tried to appease them with mixtures of honey, cream, milk, and other pleasant ingredients.

If medical science began in ancient Egypt, modern medical practice began in Greece. However, the Greeks were not all that advanced in their knowledge of anatomy and physiology. On the contrary, they knew and understood little more about the human body than their predecessors. What distinguished the Greeks from the Egyptians (and others) is that they mostly discarded magic charms and potions in favor of more practical means of treatment

Along with the disuse of magic came the awareness that all diseases have natural causes. This milestone in medical thinking is attributed to Hippocrates, a Greek physician who lived from about 460–377 BC. A collection of sixty Greek essays on medicine written at this time is called the *Hippocratic Corpus*. These almost certainly were not written by Hippocrates but apparently formed the library at his medical school. One theory set forth in them is that the body contained four fluids, or humors (blood, black and yellow bile, and phlegm).

The balances of these humors determined both a person's temperament and his health. This idea guided European medicine for the next two thousand years.

The Hippocratic Corpus contains detailed instructions for performing various surgeries, such as setting broken bones and suturing wounds, and boring holes in the skull to relieve pressure from tumors and other disorders. For many illnesses, though, Hippocrates' methods were simple and some are still in use today. He believed that one's diet played an important role in maintaining health and curing illness. His favorite medicine was honey and his favorite diet was one that consisted of barley gruel.

Hippocrates is also remembered for establishing a set of rules for doctors to follow. The Hippocratic Oath can be seen displayed in some physicians' offices today, and graduating medical students swear to uphold it when they receive their degrees. The oath stresses such standards as truthfulness, unselfishness, and devotion to duty and charges doctors to provide only helpful treatments, never doing harm, and never to divulge the secrets of their patients.

The Romans borrowed and added to what the Greeks had learned about the body and health (as the Greeks had done from the Egyptians and Mesopotamians before them). Most doctors in early Rome were, in fact, of Greek origin. The greatest of these was Galen, who lived from about AD 129–216. Some historians call Galen the "Father of Experimental Physiology." He realized that arteries carried blood (although he didn't understand how the blood circulated), and he discovered that the heart set the blood in motion. Everyone in Rome thought highly of Galen, especially

A bust of the Greek physician Hippocrates, who was the first to associate sickness with natural causes.

Galen. One of his more memorable quotes was "Whoever seeks fame need only become familiar with all that I have achieved."

In spite of the work of Galen and others, Rome's greatest contribution to health and medicine might be its achievements in sanitary engineering. Not only did the Romans build aqueducts that brought freshwater to the cities, they also had extensive sewage systems to carry off waste matter. Almost as important was their draining of swamps, which helped to control the mosquito population and the deadly diseases they transmit. Finally, the state sponsored

From *Everyday Life: Ancient Times* © 2006 Good Year Books.

medical schools, and town councils hired doctors to treat the poor, regardless of their ability to pay, thus making medicine more available to the common people.

In India, Hindu physicians acquired a knowledge of medicine that rivaled that of other civilizations. They also rejected magical explanations for illness in favor of knowledge and stressed the important of disease prevention. Ancient texts mention more than 120 surgical instruments and describe a long list of surgical procedures as well as more than five hundred herbal medicines. Indian doctors set fractures, amputated limbs, removed cataracts, did plastic surgery, and performed operations on various parts of the body. They also excelled at concocting antidotes for poisons, particularly those associated with snakebites. Many aspects of *Aruveda,* the ancient Indian system of medicine, are still practiced in India today.

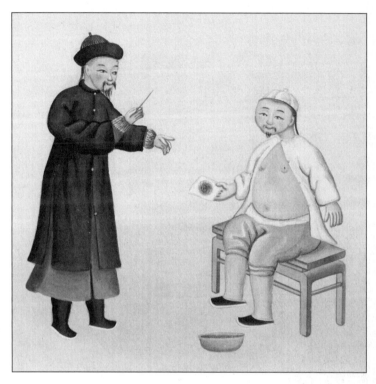

The ancient Chinese are remembered for devising acupuncture and moxibustion, which are related in principle. Acupuncture is the treatment of illness and pain by inserting needles at various points of the body. Moxibustion was a similar procedure, except that instead of needles, wicks of moxa, the pith of the Chinese wormwood tree, were burned at certain fixed points of the skin. Acupuncture and moxibustion are still performed today, especially in Asia.

Perhaps the greatest contribution of early Chinese medicine was the successful use of herbs and certain minerals for treating illnesses. Such achievements, however, were offset by a total lack of progress in sanitation and hygiene. Chinese cities and villages were plagued by improper waste disposal and the lack of clean drinking water.

A Chinese doctor prepares to treat a patient with acupuncture needles. The practice of acupuncture began in China thousands of years ago.

From *Everyday Life: Ancient Times* © 2006 Good Year Books.

Name _____ Date _____

Write Meanings of Vocabulary Words

In chapter 10, you may have read vocabulary words with which you are not familiar. Some of these you were able to understand from their context, or the way they are used in sentences. Others may not be completely clear to you.

Look up each of the following words in a dictionary and write its meaning on the lines provided. All words are nouns.

1. incantation _____

_____

2. suture _____

_____

3. diagnosis _____

_____

4. obstetrics _____

_____

5. gynecology _____

_____

6. poultice _____

_____

7. physiology _____

_____

8. gruel _____

_____

9. antidote _____

_____

10. practitioner _____

_____

From Everyday Life: Ancient Times © 2006 Good Year Books.

Name _____ Date _____

Interpret a Bar Graph

Because of primitive medical knowledge and other reasons, the average life expectancy in ancient times was low. In ancient Egypt, for example, a man could expect to live 35 years, a woman 30 years.

Life expectancies in today's world vary considerably from country to country. Much depends on a nation's standard of living, the people's level of education, and the progress it has made in health and sanitation.

The graph on this page shows the average life expectancies of six random nations in 2005. Use the information provided and answer the questions below. Write your answers on the lines following the questions.

1. What was the average life expectancy (in round numbers) of the six nations included on the graph? _____ years

2. What number represents the range of the figures shown? _____

3. U.S. citizens in 2005 could expect to live how many more years than those in Cambodia. _____

4. In which two countries is the life expectancy closest to being the same? _____ , _____

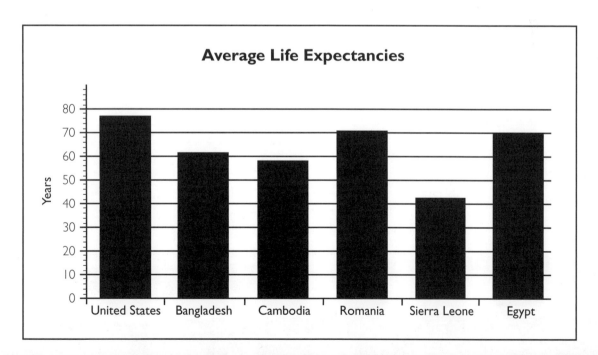

Name _____ Date _____

Create a Dialogue

For centuries ancient people believed that sickness was associated with gods or evil spirits. Then, beginning in the fifth century BC, Hippocrates and others arrived at the conclusion that all diseases have natural causes. It is easy to imagine the debate that raged throughout the civilized world with such a pronouncement.

On the lines provided, create a dialogue that might have taken place between Hippocrates and an ancient Egyptian doctor in which the former tries to convince the latter that evil spirits have nothing to do with people getting sick.

From *Everyday Life: Ancient Times* © 2006 GoodYear Books.

Name _____ Date _____

Write an Essay

Write an essay comparing and contrasting medicine (the diagnosis and treatment of disease) in ancient times with today's medical technology and procedures. Be sure to use your best grammar and sentence structure. Continue on the back of this page or on another sheet of paper, if necessary.

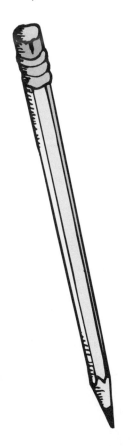

_____
_____
_____
_____
_____
_____
_____
_____
_____
_____
_____
_____
_____
_____
_____
_____
_____
_____
_____
_____
_____
_____
_____
_____
_____
_____
_____
_____
_____
_____
_____
_____
_____

CHAPTER II

Art and Architecture

If you were to travel to the Egyptian town of Giza, southwest of Cairo, you would come upon the greatest examples of what was considered one of the Seven Wonders of the Ancient World: the pyramids of Egypt. Once there were many of these royal tombs built up and down the Nile, but today there are only about eighty that remain standing. Of these, the most magnificent by far is the Great Pyramid, built in the 2400s BC for Pharaoh Khufu, or Cheops.

The Great Pyramid stands 481 feet high and covers some 13 acres. It measures more than a half mile around at the base and is large enough to cover eight football fields. All told, the structure contains more than 2,300,000 stone limestone blocks, all of which had to be transported long distances to the building site at Giza. Each block weighed at least $2\frac{1}{2}$ tons, and some, according to historians, probably weighed five times that much. More than a hundred thousand men worked from dawn to dusk for twenty or thirty years to build Khufu's tomb.

The pyramids at Gizeh. Pharaoh Khufu's pyramid is to the far right.

Some sources maintain that most of the workers at Giza were slaves. Others hold that they were peasants working to support themselves during the three-month flood season. Regardless, it is truly amazing that these laborers could move such huge blocks of stone into place and elevate them to such great heights. Historians think they accomplished this by building ramps of brick and pulling the blocks along with ropes. They may also have transported the blocks by floating them on the floodwaters of the Nile. Historians estimate that forty men were needed to move each block.

In spite of great efforts to conceal the bodies of the pharaohs in secret chambers inside their pyramids, in time grave robbers broke in and stole everything of value. Often they destroyed the bodies in the process. That is why archaeologists were ecstatic in 1922 when they discovered the intact body and treasures of Pharaoh Tutankhamen, the legendary "King Tut." His is the only tomb of an Egyptian pharaoh to be discovered that had not been tampered with by the time archaeologists discovered it.

Another architectural wonder of the Egyptians is the Great Sphinx. Also located at Giza, it is carved from solid rock at the pyramid of Khufu's son,

From *Everyday Life: Ancient Times* © 2006 Good Year Books.

Khafre. The sphinx faces the sun, and the lion is a symbol of the sun, with a sun temple at its feet. The royal human head represents the pharaoh's power and a control of the cosmic order. It measures 240 feet in length and is 66 feet wide. Its human face, which is supposed to be a likeness of Khafre himself, is more than 13 feet wide. Eighteenth-century artillerymen are blamed for using the Great Sphinx for gunnery practice and shooting off its nose—but the nose was probably gone at least four hundred years before then.

The many peoples who occupied Mesopotamia produced fine objects of gold and excelled at bas-reliefs (carvings or sculptures of figures that stand out from the background), but, like the Egyptians, they are mostly remembered for their architectural achievements. They did not build magnificent pyramids like the Egyptians, but their palaces and temples almost rival them in workmanship. The Sumerians and others are particularly associated with the construction of ziggurats, huge temple-towers in the form of a square or rectangular stepped pyramid that were scattered over the region. None of these have survived intact, but the remains of a number have been unearthed in varying conditions. You may be familiar with the Etemenanki at Babylon, which some historians maintain is the famous biblical "Tower of Babel." Little is left of it except the foundation, but from the Greek historian Herodotus's description, it must have been an imposing structure.

Herodotus visited Babylon sometime in the fifth century BC. He described the pyramid as consisting of seven levels, each recessed and smaller than the one below it. A different-colored brick was used to face each level, and at the top was a shrine furnished with a large couch and a table of gold for the god's use when he visited Earth. According to the Bible, the Tower of Babel was built by the descendants of Noah following the Great Flood. They wanted to build it to heaven, but tradition holds that God frowned on the idea and caused the builders to speak different languages, as a result of which they could not understand each other and never finished their endeavor.

Few ancient peoples could match the Greeks when it came to all forms of art, particularly drama and sculpture. The Greeks wrote and performed plays in outdoor theaters throughout the city-states, and their sculptors were the first to make their works of art realistic and lifelike. Greek plays are still performed in theaters today, and examples of their sculpture can be seen and admired in the British Museum in London and in other locations. Few examples of Greek painting have survived, but enough illustrated vases have been found that attest to the talents of Greek artists.

Greek architecture was second to none in the ancient world. Beautiful temples and public buildings built of marble and limestone dotted the countryside. Perhaps the finest example of Greek architecture is what is left of the Parthenon on the Acropolis (from the Greek words for "highest" and "city") high above the city of Athens. A closer look at this magnificent structure is worthwhile.

The Parthenon was a temple built to honor Athena, the goddess of wisdom and the patron goddess of Athens. Constructed of white marble, it was 60 feet high, 228 feet long, and 101 feet wide. All around the building were majestic columns reaching 34 feet into the air. In one of the large rooms inside was a gold and ivory statue of Athena. The statue was enormous, reaching to the ceiling and dwarfing all who came to gaze at it in awe and wonder. The statue was removed in the fifth century AD, when the Parthenon was converted to a Christian church, and it has since disappeared.

The ruins of the Parthenon, built between 447 and 432 BC, sits atop the Acropolis, a hill overlooking Athens.

The Parthenon remained essentially intact for more than two thousand years before it was reduced to its present state. It remained a temple for Athena for nearly nine hundred years, a Christian church for another thousand years, and finally a Muslim mosque for two hundred years. Then architectural disaster struck. In 1687, the Muslim Turks, who controlled Athens and who had converted the Parthenon into a powder magazine (storeroom for gunpowder), came under attack by troops from the Italian state of Venice. The Venetians lobbed a bomb that hit the structure, causing the powder magazine to go up with a roar and a large part of the walls to come down in a pile of rubble. Still, what remains of this magnificent building stands as a monument to Greek engineering and workmanship. The Lincoln Memorial in Washington, D.C., is modeled after the Parthenon.

Like the Greeks, the Romans contributed much to architecture. In addition to their aqueducts, described in a previous chapter, the Romans also built temples, palaces, law courts, amphitheaters, and triumphal arches. They made use of the arch and the vaulted dome, both of which had been unfamiliar to the Greeks. They also learned to make concrete out of lime and volcanic earth. Their buildings and other structures emphasized size rather than proportion.

From *Everyday Life: Ancient Times* © 2006 Good Year Books.

A great example of Roman architecture is the famous Colosseum in Rome. Much of it has been destroyed by earthquakes and other disasters through the years, but what remains is an imposing site. While intact, the amphitheater measured a little more than 600 feet in length and 500 feet wide. It could accommodate 50,000 spectators, who flocked there to see fights between gladiators or between men and animals. The main structure was completed in AD 80 and the uppermost deck was added in AD 82. Whereas previous amphitheaters had been built into hillsides for added support, the Colosseum was the first fully free-standing structure.

In contrast to other ancient civilizations, little is known of early Indian art. This is because Indian artists used wood, ivory, and other materials unable to withstand the ravages of time. It was not until the reign of a king named Ashoka in the third century BC that sculptors and architects began to work with more durable materials. Even then, much of what early Indian artists had created was later destroyed by Muslim conquerors in the name of religious fervor.

The Colosseum in Rome today is in ruins. In Roman times, the huge amphitheater could seat 50,000 people.

Among the best examples of Indian architecture were the many stupas that Ashoka directed to be built. Stupas were memorial shrines in the shape of hemispheres. They usually housed sacred relics related to Buddha (the founder of the religion Buddhism) and his disciples. It is said that during Ashoka's time as many as eighty-four thousand of these shrines were constructed. The most impressive stupa still standing is at Sanchi in central India.

Remains of early Chinese architecture are as scarce as those in India. Early palaces and pagodas (many-storied tower-temples derived from the Indian stupa) were all constructed of wood and rammed earth, and nothing remains of them today. The beautiful pagodas that come to mind when one thinks of the Chinese landscape were nearly all built after the fifteenth century. The oldest standing pagoda, in fact, dates only to AD 523, more than a quarter century after ancient history is said to have ended.

Chinese artists, however, excelled at metalwork and painting. Craftsmen were noted for the fine objects they turned out in bronze: masks, urns, utensils, and the like. Painters worked mostly on silk, and their artwork was as much a form of calligraphy, or beautiful penmanship, as it was painting. Chinese artists practiced for years to develop the precise, swift strokes that came to be associated with their craft.

Name _____ Date _____

Research One of the Seven Wonders

Because of space limitations, no mention was made in chapter 11 of an architectural achievement that was considered one of the Seven Wonders of the Ancient World. This was the famous Hanging Gardens of Babylon. In an encyclopedia or a book dealing with ancient history, look up the Hanging Gardens and answer the questions on this page that refer to it.

1. Which king had the Hanging Gardens of Babylon built, and why?

   _____

   _____

   _____

2. Write a description of the Hanging Gardens.

   _____

   _____

   _____

   _____

   _____

In the space below, make a sketch of the Hanging Gardens of Babylon.

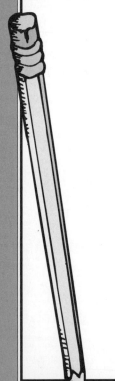

From Everyday Life: Ancient Times © 2006 Good Year Books.

Name _____ Date _____

Create a Bulletin Board Display

Have class members work together to create a bulletin board display of ancient art and architecture. Students might work separately or together drawing and coloring pictures of the following:

- The Great Pyramid at Giza
- The Great Sphinx at Giza
- The Tower of Babel (as it was thought to look)
- An Indian stupa
- The Colosseum in Rome
- A Roman aqueduct
- A Chinese pagoda
- The Parthenon

(A Teacher-directed Activity)

These are but a few examples of ancient art students can draw. Some could also sketch examples of ancient metalwork, vase and silk paintings, and other works of art. In addition to the Roman Colosseum, there is also the Circus Maximus (large, oval racetrack), which could be assigned to a student. The same holds true for examples of Greek architecture and sculpture other than the Parthenon.

You can make your bulletin board display even more comprehensive by having students draw pictures of the Seven Wonders of the Ancient World. In addition to the Pyramids of Egypt, these include the Hanging Gardens of Babylon, the Lighthouse at Alexandria, the Colossus of Rhodes, the Mausoleum at Halicarnassus, the Temple of Artemis (at Ephesus), and the Statue of Zeus (at Olympia).

Materials that will prove useful include:

1. Butcher or Kraft paper (for background)
2. Markers or crayons
3. Construction, typing, or copy paper
4. Cutout letters for the display title
5. Scissors and rulers
6. Glue or paste
7. Stapler and staples

Name _____ Date _____

Write a Letter

Pretend you are a citizen of Athens at the time the Parthenon blew up in the fighting between the Venetians and the Turks in 1687. Write a letter to a friend lamenting its partial destruction.

_____, 1687

Dear _____,

_____
_____
_____
_____
_____
_____
_____
_____
_____
_____
_____
_____
_____
_____
_____
_____
_____
_____

Your friend,

_____

(Your Name)

From Everyday Life: Ancient Times © 2006 Good Year Books.

Name _____ Date _____

Recall Information You Have Read

Without looking back over the chapter, choose the correct answer to complete each of the sentences below. Then write the answer in the blank provided.

1. Many-storied tower-temples found in China (and other Asian nations as well) are called _____.

   stupas   pagodas   pyramids

2. The pyramids of ancient Egypt were built as _____.

   temples   memorials   royal tombs

3. The Great Pyramid at Giza was built by the Pharaoh _____.

   Khafre   Khufu   Nebuchadnezzar

4. The Parthenon was built high on a hill above the city of _____.

   Rome   Sparta   Athens

5. The Great sphinx had the head of a man and the body of a _____.

   tiger   crocodile   lion

6. Memorial shrines constructed in the shape of hemispheres were called _____.

   ziggurats   stupas   pagodas

7. Aqueduct-building was an architectural activity dominated by the _____.

   Romans   Greeks   Mesopotamians

8. Huge temple-towers called *ziggurats* dotted the landscape of _____.

   India   China   Mesopotamia

9. Ashoka was a king of _____ who ruled in the third century BC.

   Egypt   Babylonia   India

10. The development of the arch and vault are associated with _____.

    China   Rome   Babylon

From *Everyday Life: Ancient Times* © 2006 Good Year Books.

Everyday Life: Ancient Times

Answers to Activities

Chapter 1

Research the Ancient World

1. Nile (Egypt), Tigris & Euphrates (Mesopotamia), Indus (India), Hwang Ho, or Yellow (China)
2. Between the rivers, or land between the rivers
3. Should include any four of the following: Sumeria, Babylonia, Assyria, and Judea (Hittites, Hebrews, Phoenicians, Chaldeans, or Persians). Other acceptable answers include Akkadians, Amorites, Elamites, Kassites, and Medes.
4. An independent state consisting of a city and its surrounding area
5. A form of government in which citizens elect representatives to make laws and to run the affairs of state
6. A group of countries or states under one ruler or government

Recall Information You Have Read

Answers should be similar to the following:
1. Engagements in most ancient societies were arranged by the parents of the bride and groom.
2. Although women in both Greece and Rome lacked political rights, women in Rome were freer to move about and to participate in social activities.
3. Women in Egypt could inherit and own property, as well as operate businesses.
4. In Greece, unwanted children could be adandoned to die, while in Mesopotamia they could be disowned by their parents or sent into exile. In China, baby girls were often left outside to die or were sometimes fed to the pigs. In contrast, children in Rome and Egypt were, for the most part, loved and cherished.

Fill in a Venn Diagram

Answers will vary but might be similar to the following:
Ancient Times: no such thing as romantic love; purpose of marriage was to have children; the father was the undisputed head of the family; women, in general, were confined to the home.
Both: families in ancient times and today had little in common; families in a few ancient societies, like today, were closely knit, and children in those societies were loved and cherished.

Today: both parents often work and share household responsibilities; young children are often left in daycare centers; there are many single-parent families.

Use Your Critical Thinking Skills

1. Answers will vary.   2. Answers will vary.
3. Men thought themselves superior to women and believed a woman's place was in the home. Women were considered property, like animals.
4. Answers will vary, especially between males and females.

Chapter 2

Use Context Clues to Complete Sentences

accommodate; feel; plight; measured; limited; little; contained; quite; modern; offset; luxury; dug; supported; apartments; better; sparsely

Distinguish between Sentences and Fragments

1. F 2. F 3. S 4. F 5. S 6. S 7. S 8. F 9. F
Sentences will vary

Solve Some Ancient Housing Word Problems

1. bedroom 2. 1,500 square feet 3. 343 square feet

Chapter 3

Solve a Clothing Puzzle

Across: 2. patrician 7. untouchables 11. sari
   13. strigil 14. palla 15. peplos
Down: 1. chlamys 3. consul 4. kohl 5. aqueduct
   6. dhoti 8. toga 9. Brahman 10. diadem
   11. chiton 12. stola

Name Those Synonyms

Sample synonyms are as follows:
1. scramble; hustle; hurry; hasten 2. recent; new; novel 3. old; aged; antique; primitive 4. look; mien; aspect; 5. copy; mimic; follow; duplicate 6. aromatic; perfumed; scented 7. resident; inhabitant; dweller 8. decorated; beautified; embellished 9. kind; sort; type 10. display; exhibit 11. gaudy; ostentatious; show-off 12. cut; lop; clip 13. main; leading; principal 14. deficit; shortfall; deficiency

From *Everyday Life: Ancient Times* © 2006 Good Year Books.

15. tool; instrument; gadget 16. stylish; chic; modish
17. clothing; garb 18. many; numberless; infinite
19. liking; inclination; taste 20. pride; conceit; smugness

Chapter 4
Make False Statements True
1. Romans and Greeks 2. Sparta 3. Romans
4. Egyptians 5. Egypt 6. Assyria 7. India
8. beer (or barley beer) 9. one-fourth 10. olives
11. two 12. milk 13. sixty 14. Roman

Search Out Some Food Facts
Answers will vary, but should include the following:
Geography: landforms, temperature, and amount of
rainfall determine what people can grow in the area;
Religion: often forbids or requires the eating of
certain foods;
Customs: what has been eaten or drunk for
generations, and the manner in which it is
consumed, often carries on;
Economy: what and how well people eat depends
on their economic condition;
Fads and Advertisement: what people see and
hear about certain foods and drink influence what
they buy and consume.

Chapter 5
Evaluate Leisure Activities
Answers will vary, but students should write and
give examples of how leisure activities are
beneficial to both physical and mental health.

Fill in a Venn Diagram
Answers will vary but might include some of the
following:
Ancient Times: hunting; banquets; athletic events;
board games; dancing
Both: hunting; athletic events; board games;
dancing; same kinds of children's games
Today: athletic events (football, basketball, baseball,
soccer, etc.); movies; TV; fairs; parties

Correct Erroneous Petronius's Math
1. 600 2. 50,000 3. 34 4. 61

Chapter 6
Name Those Ancient Persons
1. pharaoh 2. Sudra 3. patrician 4. metic
5. vizier 6. untouchable 7. plebeian 8. scribe

9. Brahman 10. optimate 11. humiliore 12. helot
13. Overseer of the Cosmetic Box 14. perioikoi
15. equestrian

Distinguish between Fact and Opinion
1. O 2. F 3. F 4. O 5. F 6. O 7. O 8. F
9. F 10. F 11. O 12. O 13. F 14. O

Chapter 7
Solve a Transportation Puzzle
1. Acta 2. chairs 3. papyrus 4. Nile 5. Persians
6. Appian 7. Hyksos 8. scribes 9. trireme
10. Canal 11. Marathon 12. Sumerians
13. holkas 14. Aegean

Chapter 8
Compare Ancient and Modern Schools
Answers will vary but should be similar to the
following:
1. School buildings: Ancient: classes often met in
   the street or at the teacher's home; Modern:
   comfortable, air-conditioned classrooms;
2. Subjects taught: Ancient: writing, logic,
   arithmetic, history, geography, etc.; Modern:
   well-rounded curriculum, including advanced
   courses in science and mathematics;
3. Purpose of education: Ancient: to prepare
   students to become scribes, priests, etc.;
   Modern: prepare students for life and a career;
4. Who attended: Ancient: mostly children of the
   upper classes; Modern: all children;
5. Teachers: Ancient: usually priests or educated
   slaves; Modern: trained, certified teachers;
6. Discipline: Ancient: very harsh; students often
   severely beaten; Modern: corporal punishment
   seldom used today;
7. Education for girls: Ancient: most girls were
   educated at home to perform domestic duties;
   Modern: girls receive the same education as
   boys;
8. Students' ages: Ancient: usually from about 7 to
   13–16; Modern: 5 to 17–18;
9. Teaching methods: Ancient: lecture; rote;
   Modern: various methods used

Unscramble and Identify Nouns
1. HIEROGLYPHICS, Egyptian form of picture
writing 2. GURU, religious teacher of ancient India
3. CUNEIFORM, wedge-shaped writing used in

Mesopotamia 4. STYLUS, writing tool
5. ASHURBANIPAL, Assyrian king who built a
great library at Ninevah 6. PAIDEGOGOS, slave
who accompanied boys to school 7. SUDRA, serf
of ancient India 8. POLYTHEISM, belief in many
gods 9. POSEIDON, Greek god of the sea
10. HINDUISM, a religion of India 11. APHRODITE,
Greek goddess of love and beauty

Chapter 9
Make False Statements True
1. harsh 2. cuneiform 3. Ten Commandments
4. lawmakers 5. bronze 6. Forum 7. varied
from class to class 8. Roman 9. Brass 10. Roman
11. the emperor 12. jury 13. more

Chapter 10
Write Meanings of Vocabulary Words
1. words spoken as a magic charm or to cast a
spell 2. seam formed in sewing up a wound
3. the identification of a disease by careful
examination of its symptoms 4. branch of medicine
concerned with treating women before, during,
and after childbirth 5. branch of medicine dealing
with the treatment of women's diseases 6. a soft,
moist, hot mass of various products applied to a
sore or infected part of the body 7. branch of
science dealing with the functions of living things
or their parts 8. thin broth made by cooking meal
in water or milk 9. a remedy to counteract the
effects of a poison 10. person engaged in the
practice of a profession

Interpret a Bar Graph
1. 64 2. 34 3. 19 4. Romania and Egypt

Chapter 11
Research One of the Seven Wonders
1. Nebuchadnezzar II, because his wife was
    homesick for the mountain scenery of her
    native land (also sometimes attributed to
    Queen Sammu-ramat).
2. The Hanging Gardens were a series of root
    gardens built on the terraces of a ziggurat.
    Man-made waterfalls fell from one level to the
    next. The gardens were said to "hang" because
    flowers and vines grew over the edges of the
    terraces.

Recall Information You Have Read
1. pagodas 2. royal tombs 3. Khufu 4. Athens
5. lion 6. stupas 7. Romans 8. Mesopotamia
9. India 10. Rome

Additional Resources (Selected)

Books for Children
Landau, Elaine. *The Assyrians.* Brookfield, Connecticut:
    Millbrook Press, 1997.
Langley, Andrew, and Philip de Souza. *The Roman
    News.* Cambridge, Massachusetts:
    Candlewick Press, 1996.
Millard, Anne. *Ancient Egypt.* New York: Warwick
    Press, 1979.
Odjik, Pamela. *The Romans.* Englewood Cliffs, New
    Jersey: Silver Burdett Press, 1989.
Powell, Anton, and Philip Steele. *The Greek News.*
    Cambridge, Massachusetts: Candlewick
    Press, 2000.

Books for Adults
Balsdon, J. P. V. D. *Life and Leisure in Ancient Rome.*
    London: Phoenix Press, 2004.
Budge, E. A. Wallis. *Babylonian Life and History.*
    New York: Barnes and Noble Books, 2005.
Connolly, Peter, and Hazel Dodge. *The Ancient City:
    Life in Classical Athens & Rome.* Oxford:
    Oxford University Press, 2000.
Martin, Thomas R. *Ancient Greece.* New Haven,
    Connecticut: Yale University Press, 2000.
Shaw, Ian. *The Oxford History of Ancient Egypt.*
    Oxford: Oxford University Press, 2002.

From *Everyday Life: Ancient Times* © 2006 Good Year Books.